Forbidden Wars

The Unwritten Rules that Keep Us Safe

Theodore Caplow

UNIVERSITY PRESS OF AMERICA,® INC.
Lanham • Boulder • New York • Toronto • Plymouth, UK

Copyright © 2007 by
University Press of America,® Inc.
4501 Forbes Boulevard
Suite 200
Lanham, Maryland 20706
UPA Acquisitions Department (301) 459-3366

Estover Road
Plymouth PL6 7PY
United Kingdom

Library of Congress Control Number: 2007926016
ISBN-13: 978-0-7618-3570-4 (paperback : alk. paper)
ISBN-10: 0-7618-3570-5 (paperback : alk. paper)

$\bigotimes^{TM}$ The paper used in this publication meets the minimum
requirements of American National Standard for Information
Sciences—Permanence of Paper for Printed Library Materials,
ANSI Z39.48—1992

Contents

Preface   v

1 Nuclear Rules   1

2 Since Hiroshima   5

3 Nuclear Decisions   10

4 Nuclear Strategies   20

5 Non-Events   31

6 The Nuclear Taboo   40

7 Hostages and Tripwires   51

8 Nuclear Restraints   57

9 Regulating War   68

10 Low-Intensity Conflict   79

11 The Imperial Project   85

12 Post-Imperial Opportunities   92

13 Safer Than It Seems   97

14 Postcript   101

Contents

Notes	103
Reference	109
About the Author	117

Preface

As a young soldier I visited the still-smoking ruins of Hiroshima and the images of that unhappy place have been in the back of my mind ever since, not only as a painful memory but as an intellectual challenge that remains unsolved to this day. The war we were winning by normal means was abruptly transposed into science-fiction. The atom bomb fractured the balance between attack and defense that had governed human conflict since the dawn of history. As there could be no effective defense against a nuclear attack, social and political institutions, particularly those regarding armed conflict, would have to be changed to prevent nuclear attacks from happening.

As will be seen in the following pages, the solution initially proposed was the abolition of international war but that solution proved to be incompatible with the existing pattern of international relations and the normal prerogatives of nation-states. What developed instead, after much strategic fumbling, was an arrangement whereby nuclear attacks are prevented by the deployment of large numbers of nuclear weapons by hostile and potentially hostile powers which can show a convincing intention to use them if sufficiently provoked.

This mechanism, known as nuclear deterrence, has been surprisingly effective so far, despite numerous false alarms and close calls, but it is can not be safely viewed as a permanent solution to the problem of preventing the actual use of nuclear weapons. In a book called *Peace Games,* published a few months before the collapse of the Soviet Union, I called attention to the fact that while war games envisaging conflicts with every conceivable adversary are played incessantly by the military and naval staffs of nuclear-armed nations, there is no corresponding tradition of peace games, either in the corridors of power or among civilian strategists. Not a thousandth of the mental effort devoted to war games is available to considering options for the long-term prevention of nuclear war and nuclear terrorism.

Peace Games was just such an exercise, but after reviewing the available alternatives, I was forced to admit that none of them seemed feasible in the short run under then existing conditions. What I hope to show in *Forbidden Wars* is that it has now become possible to describe better solutions to the problem of preventing nuclear war than the mindless pursuit of strategic advantage. There are opportunities now that were not there before and this is a good time to examine them.

T.C.
Dark Harbor, Maine
July 2006

Chapter One

Nuclear Rules

More than sixty years have passed since the detonation of the first atomic bomb. It was widely believed at the time that nuclear weapons would make war impossible. That belief was abandoned in the second half of the twentieth century when dozens of little wars were fought in the shadow of the unfightable Cold War. Yet the belief held more than a grain of truth. No war has occurred so far between nuclear-armed states and none is likely to occur. Three unwritten and largely unrecognized rules have governed international relations in the nuclear era:

Rule One: A non-nuclear state must not attack a nuclear state with its national forces.

Rule Two: A nuclear state must not attack another nuclear state with its national forces.

Rule Three: Any state may attack a non-nuclear state with its national forces, if the defending state has no nuclear guarantor.

These rules were never formally proposed or enacted, but they command stricter compliance than any of the older rules of war established by treaty or custom, and their unbroken self-enforcement has created a strong taboo against any military use of nuclear weapons, even those uses that the rules would permit.

The only exceptions to perfect compliance to Rule One during the past sixty years were the intervention of Chinese forces in the Korean War, which was not viewed as an attack on the U.S, since the forces defending South Korea fought under the UN flag; the firing of Iraqi scuds against Israel during the first Gulf War, which by agreement between the U.S. and Israel, was treated as an incident in the permissible Rule Three conflict between the U.S. and Iraq, and some border skirmishes between Russian and Chinese troops on the remote eastern borders of the Soviet Union, which were quickly suppressed by both governments.

The rules enforced themselves in every close call of the Cold War—the flock of geese crossing the DEW line that radar mistook for a flock of missiles, the Berlin airlift, the Cuban missile crisis, the war game that found its way into a Pentagon early warning computer. More recently, the rules pulled India and Pakistan back from the brink in Kashmir. And they have prevailed over innumerable glitches and accidents in the systems designed to prevent accidental launches.

The nuclear rules did not result in the abolition of war. As it happened, more wars were fought in the second half of the twentieth century than in any previous half-century, all of them permissible under the rules. Yet there are significant degrees of freedom in these rules. They would allow the United States to disengage not only from the occupation of Iraq but from other military commitments without jeopardizing national security.

At the very beginning of the nuclear age, the decision to use the atom bomb against a Japanese city was made without extended reflection. As Secretary of War Stimson later wrote, "At no time, from 1941 to 1945, did I ever hear it suggested by the President, or by any other responsible member of the government, that atomic energy should not be used in the war . . . [it] was considered to be . . . as legitimate as any other of the deadly explosive weapons of modern war." [1] Thus, the bomb was defined administratively as just a new type of Air Force ordnance. The committee appointed to consider nuclear options in 1945 was made up of three statesmen and three scientific luminaries. The four members of their advisory panel were the country's most eminent physicists.[2] After discussion with the panel, the committee recommended that the bomb should be used against Japan, on a "military target surrounded by houses" and that it should be dropped without warning.[3] Stimson did intervene to veto the selection of Kyoto as a target, partly because of its cultural and artistic significance and partly because he feared that the bitterness caused by its loss might incline the postwar Japanese to prefer Russian to American occupiers. So Hiroshima was destroyed by a single bomb and Nagasaki met the same fate three days later. Nagasaki in ruins never aroused wide interest but the image of blasted and blackened Hiroshima seemed to sink into humanity's collective psyche and exert an uncanny influence from there. Since then, innumerable military and civilian strategists have challenged Rules One and Two and insisted on the wisdom and necessity of putting nuclear weapons to work.[4] Indeed, by a paradox that lies at the heart of the matter, nuclear deterrence works only because the possessors of nuclear weapons are convincingly ready to fire them off under sufficient provocation.

But somehow, against all probability, not a single nuclear weapon has been fired in anger since August of 1945. Not only has the deterrence of wars that would fall under Rules One and Two been conspicuously effective. The deep fear that nuclear weapons inspire seems to have prevented nuclear accidents and even to have discouraged nuclear terrorism.

I am fully aware that this favorable situation may change before this book is printed, or next year or the year after, but if that were to happen, the world's sixty-year abstention from the use of nuclear weapons would still, even in retrospect, deserve examination.

The discussion of deterrence in this book refers only to nuclear weapons, not to biological and chemical weapons, The conflation of nuclear explosives, man-made epidemics and poison gas into weapons of mass destruction (WMD) was the style adopted by the Bush administration in making a case for the invasion of Iraq, perhaps because it was known that the Iraqis had once had abundant supplies of biological and chemical agents and equally certain that they had not succeeded in developing nuclear weapons.

The WMD usage invites confusion. There can be no possible question about the vast damage that can be inflicted by nuclear explosives. Biological and chemical weapons have no such demonstrated potential. The unexplained anthrax attack that followed September 11 caused great alarm in Washington and shut down important government buildings but caused, in the end, just five deaths. Smallpox has been touted as an irresistible plague, but vaccination is an adequate defense and even if a worse plague were disseminated, experience with Ebola and SARS indicates that the spread of a lethal contagious disease can be checked by taking reasonable measures.

Poison gas, first used on the western front of World War I in 1916 by the Germans and then by the Allies, was eventually recognized as more of a nuisance than an asset on the battlefield. More recently, it has been tried out on helpless villagers in Ethiopia and Iraq, and on unsuspecting commuters in the Tokyo subway but its military utility is limited.

While the abolition of nuclear weapons is not likely to get serious consideration any time soon, the abolition of biological and chemical weapons by international treaty is well under way, despite considerable resistance. At least for the time being, the weapons of mass destruction that matter are nuclear.

The evolution of the American nuclear arsenal included one choice point after another, each marked by controversies among defense intellectuals and policy-makers as they tried to devise a formula for winning a nuclear war against the Soviet Union. That effort drove them irresistibly towards worst-case scenarios, in which the United States never achieved the superiority of force necessary to check the Soviet Union's drive for world domination. At every choice point, the debate ended with a decision to escalate the nuclear competition, going from fission weapons to fusion weapons, from kilotons to megatons, from planes to missiles, from single to multiple warheads, from approximate to precision aiming.

These habits of mind were formed in the 1950s when the Soviet Union had taken control of eastern Europe, the communist bloc was unbroken, and communist parties were thriving in western Europe. The rift between China and the Soviet Union in 1959 was the first of many cracks in that formidable façade. But the illusion that the balance of power favored the Soviet Union over the United States persisted in some quarters until the fall of the Berlin Wall.

When the Soviet Union shrank into the Russian Federation and became a client and "strategic partner" of the United States, the rationale of the nuclear confrontation disappeared but the missiles remained in place. Today, the sole superpower and the ex-superpower continue to confront each other with thousands of nuclear weapons, for reasons seldom debated. This situation makes no strategic sense and carries grave risks.

Chapter Two

Since Hiroshima

At Hiroshima on the morning of August 6, 1945, a single U.S. Air Force plane demolished a city and killed most of its inhabitants with an atom bomb. At Los Alamos that same afternoon, the scientists who had built the weapon were jubilant. "The place went up like we won the Army-Navy game," said one physicist. Another described the behavior of J. Robert Oppenheimer, the project's scientific director and moving spirit, as he mounted the stage. "He entered the meeting like a prizefighter." And clasped his hands over his head in a boxer's victory salute.[5]

The political leaders who had made it all possible were equally jubilant. Public opinion was thoroughly supportive. Moral objections were few and faint.[6] A Gallup poll on August 26 found that 85 percent of those surveyed endorsed the atomic attacks.

In March of that same year, hundreds of American planes had rained incendiary bombs on Tokyo. The death toll was greater than it would be at Hiroshima. In July, American planes burned sixty-six other Japanese cities. A few, including Hiroshima, were deliberately spared for later use as targets.

On August 9, a second and more powerful atom bomb was dropped on Nagasaki. After that city was selected, someone reported that American prisoners of war were detained there. That uncomfortable fact was not allowed to interfere with the targeting decision.[7]

The initial euphoria soon gave way to a protracted debate about the wisdom and morality of the decision to use the bomb against the two Japanese cities without warning or demonstration. That debate continues to this day.[8] On one side are those who insist that the destruction of Hiroshima and Nagasaki brought on a Japanese surrender that might otherwise have required a costly invasion of the home islands. On the other side are those who maintain that Japan had exhausted its military resources and was ready to surrender without an invasion.

Some of the Manhattan Project scientists who built the bomb had the earliest qualms. Before the attack on Hiroshima, Leo Szilard—the physicist who had first envisaged the atom bomb—circulated a petition among his colleagues urging the President to demonstrate the new weapon to the Japanese on a desert or an uninhabited island before using it on live people. The petition, signed by 155 Manhattan Project scientists, was deliberately bottled up in the chain of command[9] and never reached the White House.

Sixty years of research and discussion have produced a consensus among historians that the war could have been ended in a relatively short time without using the new weapons and without an invasion. The general public, however, seems still to accept the official position of 1945 - that the two atomic bombs avoided an invasion that would have cost hundreds of thousands of American lives.

Walker[10] lists the motives behind the decision to employ the new weapons: ending the war at the earliest possible moment; justifying the cost of the Manhattan project; intimidating the Soviet Union; taking vengeance against the perpetrators of Pearl Harbor and the Bataan Death March; and perhaps most important, the absence of any strong incentive to desist.

Two months before the bombing of Hiroshima, scientists working for the Manhattan Project at the University of Chicago had submitted a report to Secretary Stimson warning about an atomic arms race and proposing that the bomb be demonstrated to international observers on a desert or an uninhabited island. Called the Franck report, it was eventually delivered to the Secretary's office by Arthur Compton, who, in his covering letter, dismissed the proposal for a peaceful demonstration with the argument that if the bomb were not used in the current war, the world would not be adequately warned against any future war. Since it was a common belief among the scientists who created the bomb was that war had been made impossible, many of them favored its use in the closing days of the war with Japan on the theory that a bloodless demonstration might not be equally effective in preventing future wars.

This was the view of James B. Conant, distinguished chemist, president of Harvard and the principal recruiter of scientists for the Manhattan Project[11] and of Stimson's scientific advisors when they rejected the Franck report in favor of "direct military use." They may not have been entirely wrong. War was not abolished but many imaginable wars were ruled out by nuclear deterrence, and they were the wars with the greatest potential damage.

The bombing of Hiroshima and Nagasaki might have caused more of a moral recoil in the U.S. had not the firebombing of Tokyo a few months before caused death and destruction on an even greater scale, and the earlier firebombing of Hamburg and Dresden accustomed public opinion to the massacre of enemy civilians.

The concerns of statesmen in the victor nations were strategic rather than moral.

Prior to the experimental test of the atom bomb at Alamogordo, the Truman administration had been trying to bring the Soviet Union into the war against Japan. After that demonstration, the aim was to keep them out. Although the Soviet Union declared war on Japan and invaded Manchuria just after the bombing of Hiroshima, it was not invited to participate in the surrender and occupation of Japan. When the news of Alamogordo reached the President at the Potsdam conference:

> .... Truman strolled over to Stalin with an air of studied nonchalance and mentioned that the United States had developed new weapons of "unusual destructive force." Stalin, according to Truman's memoirs, replied that he was pleased to hear of it and hoped that the President "would make good use of it against the Japanese." Byrnes and Churchill, who watched the conversation from a distance, were surprised and gratified that Stalin seemed to take so little interest in Truman's report. [12]

They did not know that Stalin was fully informed about the Manhattan Project thanks to Klaus Fuchs and other spies, and had ordered the Soviet nuclear program into high gear. The Cold War was just down the road.

Seven great powers had entered World War II between 1939 and 1941—Germany, France, Great Britain, the Soviet Union, Italy, Japan and the U.S. Germany had the strongest army and air force. The U.S. and Great Britain had the largest navies, with Japan, France and Italy not far behind. The Soviet Union had huge but poorly equipped ground forces. No other national state had any significant warmaking capacity.

The fortunes of war finished Japan and Germany as great powers and gravely weakened France and Italy. Britain declined more slowly as its overseas possessions peeled away and it became a military satellite of the U.S.The responsibility for adjusting the international war system to the existence of nuclear weapons after World War II thus fell to the U.S. and the Soviet Union. At first, that responsibility seemed to be taken seriously. Five months after the bombing of Hiroshima and Nagasaki the American, British and Soviet foreign ministers met in Moscow and drafted a resolution calling for a commission to propose "the elimination from national armaments of atomic weapons and all other major weapons adaptable to mass destruction." The resolution passed unanimously at the very first meeting of the General Assembly of the United Nations at Lake Success. President Truman then chose Bernard Baruch to negotiate an agreement with the Soviets. Baruch was a retired Wall Street speculator who had played an important role in mobilizing the American economy for World War I and had served as a political guru for several presidents. He was technologically ignorant and bitterly anti-Soviet.[13]

The proposal Baruch submitted to the United Nations a few months later called for an International Atomic Development Authority which would control all atomic activity, including the manufacture of weapons, research and development, and the discovery of peaceful uses. It would control uranium and thorium in the ground as well as stockpiles of raw and processed radioactive materials, would have inspection rights throughout the world, and would exercise criminal jurisdiction over atomic offenders. Existing atomic weapons would eventually be turned over to the Authority. None would remain under the control of a national government. Any violation of the Authority's regulations would be met with "condign punishment"—a favorite phrase of Baruch, which was understood to mean that the violator would suffer an atomic attack.

At the time, the U.S. possessed all of the existing atomic weapons. No one knew how long it would take the Soviet Union to catch up; some estimates ran to decades. To Americans, the offer to transfer the American monopoly to a neutral international agency seemed generous and even rash.

What the Soviet representatives thought they saw was a plot to perpetuate the American monopoly. The details of the Baruch Plan fueled their suspicions. The U.S. would surrender its atomic holdings to the Authority on a schedule of its own choosing while the Authority's inspectors would take immediate control of Soviet atomic installations. Baruch sought no compromise and hastened to report failure. The Soviets tested an atomic bomb of their own in 1949 and the nuclear arms race was on.

Chapter Three

Nuclear Decisions

J. Robert Oppenheimer's[14] jubilation about the bombing of Hiroshima was short-lived. Only three days after the Japanese surrender, he was drafting a letter to Secretary of War Stimson to say that the nation had no defense against the new weapons and no hope of monopolizing them. When he carried the letter to Washington, he found that the President had issued a gag order on any further disclosures about the atomic bomb and that Secretary of State Byrnes wanted to push ahead with its development without delay.

Oppenheimer was now world-famous and the nation harkened to his every word. Within weeks he was saying that the Hiroshima bomb used "against an essentially defeated enemy . . . is a weapon for aggressors . . . and the elements of surprise and terror are as intrinsic to it as are the fissionable nuclei."[15] This was strong language from the man who had recommended that the bomb be used on a Japanese city without a warning but more contradictions were to come.

When the issue of managing the new weapons came before Congress in October 1945, it took the form of the May-Johnson bill, which proposed to centralize authority over atomic matters in a nine-member commission, including military officers. It would have sent scientists to prison for even minor security violations. To the surprise of his colleagues, Oppenheimer supported the measure on the ground that it would pave the way for an international agreement. Nonetheless, energetic lobbying by other scientists defeated the bill. The atomic control legislation eventually adopted provided for a civilian commission but subjected nuclear scientists to tight security regulations, thus installing the regime of secrecy that surrounds nuclear weapons to this day.

Dismayed by the rumblings about a possible war with the Soviet Union, Oppenheimer asked and obtained an interview with President Truman in October 1945. It turned out badly when Oppenheimer told the president that he felt he had blood on his hands. An infuriated Truman, rejecting the thought of blood on his own hands, was quoted as saying, "I don't want to see that sonofabitch in this office ever again."[16]

Shortly afterward, J. Edgar Hoover, the powerful director of the FBI, began to circulate derogatory information about Oppenheimer's youthful contacts with West Coast communists to the White House and the State Department. Oppenheimer would remain under FBI surveillance for the rest of his public career, trailed by phalanxes of agents who opened his mail, tapped his phones and recorded family conversations. The thousands of pages in his FBI file have been a rich source for his biographers.

In January 1946, Oppenheimer was heartened by the President's appointment of a special committee to draw up a proposal for the international control of nuclear weapons, under the chairmanship of Dean Acheson, who quickly named a Board of consultants headed by Oppenheimer. Within two months the Board of Consultants was ready with a long draft report calling for an international agency that would control all aspects of atomic energy and distribute the benefits to individual countries. No individual nation would be permitted to build or hold bombs. All of the agency's operations would be totally transparent— there would be no classified documents in its domain. The report, mostly written by Oppenheimer, was known as the Acheson-Lilienthal report. It shocked Secretary of State Byrnes who prevailed on the president to designate Baruch to carry the proposal to the United Nations, with the result already mentioned.

Oppenheimer was crushed. He was sure that if there were another major war, nuclear weapons would be used, if only because he himself had advocated their use against an enemy he now described as having been "essentially defeated" at the time. But by late 1947, he had persuaded himself that the Soviets were not likely to agree to international control and he began to quietly support the mass production of nuclear weapons by the U.S.

Meanwhile, Lewis Strauss, who was both a member of the Atomic Energy Commission and a trustee of the Institute for Advanced Study in Princeton, offered the directorship of the Institute to Oppenheimer, who accepted with pleasure. Strauss would become Oppenheimer's bitter enemy after repeated clashes about institute politics.

In 1949, Oppenheimer was subpoenaed by the notorious House Committee on Un-American Activities and shocked his friends by testifying about the leftist associations of former students and colleagues.

When the Soviet Union tested its first atom bomb in August 1949, Oppenheimer hoped it would persuade Truman to change course and pursue the project of international control. Instead, Truman listened to the Joint Chiefs of Staff and authorized a six-fold increase in the nuclear arsenal while Strauss circulated a memo lamenting the loss of America's nuclear monopoly and arguing for the development of a thermonuclear or hydrogen bomb, which would go beyond nuclear fission to nuclear fusion—a project that Oppenheimer had opposed since 1945. Oppenheimer promptly convened a meeting of his advisory committee where a consensus against the hydrogen bomb developed. The President, however, had already made up his mind and announced that the U.S. would proceed to explore the technical feasibility of thermonuclear weapons.

The decision to develop the hydrogen bomb was made over the objections of such influential figures as George Kennan and James Conant. They argued that the innovation was unnecessary, that it would put a stop to the fading hope of international control and that the threat to develop it could be used to negotiate restraint with the Soviets, who had just tested their first fission weapon. The moral argument that had been deferred since Hiroshima also raised its feeble head. Fusion weapons would be even more obviously directed against noncombatants than fission weapons. With no upper limit to their explosive yield, they would bring a Doomsday bomb into the realm of the possible. None of these arguments had much weight against the prospect of additional nuclear assets. [17]

From that point on, Oppenheimer was the victim of a campaign orchestrated by two people with hurt feelings: Lewis Strauss and Edward Teller. It took them some time to bring him down, renewing old charges that had been reviewed and dismissed many times before but adding the new charge of insufficient enthusiasm for thermonuclear weapons. A proposal for a thermonuclear moratorium submitted to the National Security Council in 1952 by Oppenheimer's panel was curtly rejected and within a month the United States exploded a 10.4-megaton thermonuclear bomb, with nearly a thousand times the explosive power of the Hiroshima bomb on the Pacific island of Elugelap, which disappeared without a trace.

In 1954, during the Eisenhower administration, Strauss, by then chairman of the Atomic Energy Commission, organized a protracted hearing to review Oppenheimer's security clearance. There was no pretense of due process. Oppenheimer's conferences with his lawyers were secretly recorded. The hearing panel was provided with documents that the defense was not allowed to examine. Edward Teller, the strongest advocate of the hydrogen bomb, testified against his former patron. After weeks of slanted testimony, the panel ruled that the father of the atomic bomb was a loyal citizen but also a security risk. And the mass production of nuclear warheads moved into high gear.

During his eight years as president, Dwight D. Eisenhower successively occupied all of the major positions on nuclear strategy that have been debated in the upper echelons of the federal government ever since. In his 1952 campaign, he promised to put a quick end to the Korean War and when he came into office, he repeatedly asked the Air Force to develop a plan that would end the war by means of a nuclear assault on the North Koreans. Barely seven years into the nuclear age, he called on them to abandon the "nuclear tabu."

In May 1953, he approved a contingency plan to renew the ground offensive in Korea along with nuclear strikes against Chinese air bases in Manchuria. Afterwards, Eisenhower and his Secretary of State, John Foster Dulles, believed that their willingness to break the nuclear taboo and the warnings they transmitted to China and North Korea through back channels had made it possible to negotiated a durable cease-fire in Korea. They may have been mistaken in this judgment, since the Chinese apparently relied on their 1950 alliance with the nuclear-armed Soviet Union as sufficient protection against American nuclear strikes and had other reasons for accepting a truce.[18] But only a year later, when the U.S. and its allies considered intervening in Vietnam to turn the tide at Dien Bien Phu, Eisenhower rejected proposals from some of his military advisers to threaten the use of tactical nuclear weapons.

Although by then both the U.S. and the Soviet Union had already run successful thermonuclear tests, it seems to have been operation BRAVO in 1954 that persuaded Eisenhower to abandon the idea of limited nuclear war and support the taboo.[19] BRAVO was a thermonuclear test that got out of hand. Its explosion, hundreds of times more powerful than that of the Hiroshima bomb, was much greater than expected and its fallout contaminated a large section of the Pacific Ocean.

Eisenhower now concluded that the a limited nuclear war would be difficult, if not impossible, to contain, and directed the Pentagon to compare for a total nuclear war on the theory that the Soviet government would neither initiate a nuclear conflict nor take actions provocative enough to invite a nuclear first strike by the United States, since in either case such actions would amount to national suicide.

Since the requirement for a convincing threat of total war in the 1950s was an indisputable ability to destroy the Soviet Union, and since it was taken for granted in Washington that a Soviet first strike was more likely than an American first strike, Eisenhower's next strategy called for the maintenance of an unchallengeable second-strike capability—that is, the capability to absorb a Soviet first strike and then to respond with a second strike that would reliably devastate the enemy. Since neither the scale nor the effectiveness of the Soviet first strike could be reliably predicted, the new strategy called for the production of so many nuclear warheads that even if most of them were lost in absorbing the first strike, those remaining would be amply sufficient to obliterate all of the Soviet cities and any military assets they retained.

Throughout Eisenhower's presidency, the chosen adversary was not the Soviet Union alone but the Soviet Union plus the People's Republic of China plus East Germany plus the other member states of the Warsaw Pact. The Communist bloc was regarded in Washington as a unified entity governed from Moscow. The Single Integrated Operational Plan or SIOP that Eisenhower left for Kennedy envisaged a preemptive nuclear attack that would deliver more than 3000 nuclear weapons on more than 2000 targets in all of the countries with communist regimes. It was expected to produce more than 300 million deaths. Towards the end of Eisenhower's second term, the United States was manufacturing ten nuclear bombs a day.[20]

Although the public was given to understand that only the President could authorize a nuclear strike, it later became known that Eisenhower "predelegated" military commanders to exercise that authority independently if (1) attacks on U.S. territory and possessions provided no time for consultation with the President or (2) enemy attacks prevented a presidential decision. Recently reclassified documents disclose the chronology of predelegation.[21] Beginning in 1956, the instructions became more and more elaborate and the list of predelegated commanders became longer and longer. Kennedy let these instructions stand and Johnson in 1964 approved a revision. The subsequent history of predelegation is still classified but it is clear that through much of the Cold War the nuclear option was equipped with a hair trigger, which makes the nuclear restraint that prevailed even more remarkable.

Most of the foreign crises that preoccupied Eisenhower's administration were in Asia rather than Europe—especially the winding down of the Korean War, the protection of Taiwan from a Chinese invasion, and the crises over Quemoy and Matsu provoked by Mao Tse-Tung in 1954-55 and renewed by him in 1958.

Yet when it came to nuclear policy, the reliance on total nuclear war to defer the communists in the later years of the Eisenhower administration was confined to the European theater. Threats of limited nuclear war seemed more appropriate for deterring the Chinese from invading Taiwan or seizing the offshore islands and were used freely for that purpose. The administration went so far as to equip Chiang's Kai-Shek's forces on Taiwan with middle-range nuclear weapons and to threaten nuclear strikes throughout both crises. At one point in 1958, the British took pains to inform Washington that they did not think that the islands in the Taiwan Strait were worth a world war.[22]

Eisenhower the general was in some ways the least militaristic president from Truman to G. W. Bush, as shown by the grim warning about the undue influence of the military-industrial complex that was the theme of his farewell address and by his famous "cross of iron" speech:

> Every gun that is made, every warship launched, every rocket fired signifies . . . a theft from those who hunger and are not fed, those who are cold and not clothed. The world in arms is not spending money alone. It is spending the sweat of its laborers, the genius of its scientists, the hopes of its children. The cost of one modern bomber is this: a modern brick school in more than 30 cities . . . two fine fully equipped hospitals. This is not a way of life at all . . . It is humanity hanging from a cross of iron. [23]

And although it is hard to imagine today, Eisenhower's great enlargement of the country's nuclear arsenal in the 1950s was conceived as an economy measure, enabling him to reduce the size of the armed services and to discourage expensive military research and development. He was acutely aware that the cost of destroying lives and structures by nuclear explosives was almost negligible compared to the cost of doing it with conventional weapons and that appealed both to his fiscal conservatism and his distrust of defense contractors. Yet the long-term effect of his mixed nuclear policies was to raise the Cold War to a higher pitch and lay the groundwork for the largest military establishment in history.

By what they did and what they were unable to do, Oppenheimer and Eisenhower set the pattern of war and peace in the nuclear age. Unlike in most respects, they resembled each other in their inability to choose between incompatible positions about the use of nuclear weapons.

So Oppenheimer could celebrate the bombing of Hiroshima when it occurred and denounce it a few weeks later as an act of aggression against an essentially defeated enemy. He could both oppose and support the development of the hydrogen bomb, both oppose and support secrecy in atomic matters, both oppose and support the views of Manhattan project scientists on the utilization of what they had invented.

Eisenhower, for his part, settled on a policy of limited nuclear war, then opted for the deterrent effect of total nuclear war, then threatened limited nuclear war. He opposed a military buildup and presided over a huge expansion of offensive capability.

They were both thoughtful men, with wider views than most of their professional colleagues. But in the end, their preferences were too unfocused to prevail against the momentum of a military establishment energized by a recent victory, a plausible adversary and the conundrum of weapons too powerful to be used.

The Cold War between the United States and the Soviet Union was fully engaged by 1948. Moscow's announced intention was to control and communize the whole world. The project seemed to be making a good start in eastern Europe and the Red Army was thought to be poised for the conquest of Western Europe. [24] Washington had a monopoly of nuclear weapons, the planes to deliver them and an announced willingness to use them on Moscow and Leningrad. Each side looked intolerably threatening to the other. During the next twenty-five years, the mutual threats became more symmetrical as both the ground forces and the nuclear arsenals approached parity. But old fears died hard. Each side continued to feel intolerably threatened. As late as the 1980s, with the Soviet Union on its last legs, some American strategists were still deploring an imaginary Soviet advantage in military strength. [25]

Indeed, U.S. intelligence agencies and civilian strategists consistently overestimated Soviet capacities throughout the Cold War. This was understandable on the part of the CIA and other elements of the official intelligence community. Their function was to issue warnings and no particular harm would be done if the warnings were exaggerated, whereas a failure to warn sufficiently might be disastrous. The same tendency colored the vast literature of strategic studies, which contained innumerable overestimates of Soviet strength and no underestimates to speak of, although for an additional reason. Because most strategic studies relied implicitly on game theory, they tended to reduce the motivation of "players" to "winning" without regard to the complexity of real life motives. These two sources of error converged so that in almost all discussion of U.S. nuclear options between 1949 and 1989, the Soviet leadership was depicted as implausibly risk-acceptant. Thus, Secretary McNamara's 1966 budget statement to Congress estimated that the Soviet Union could be effectively deterred by the loss of one quarter to one third of its population and two-thirds of its industrial capacity.[26] There was a clear implication that the destruction of less than a quarter of the Soviet population would not be something their leaders would try to avoid.

The three nuclear rules appeared as soon as the Soviet Union acquired its first atomic bomb. Rule Two was interpreted as prohibiting the conventional forces of a nuclear state from engaging in armed conflict with the conventional forces of another nuclear state. This interpretation allowed the Cold War to be waged without a direct confrontation of the principal parties. During the Cold War an armed conflict anywhere in the world invited the participation of both the U.S. and the Soviet Union, and both routinely accepted such invitations, sending funds, supplies and, on occasion, troops, to their chosen proxies. But since any direct U.S. action against Soviet troops, or Soviet actions against U.S. troops, might be construed as a violation of Rule Two, each side scrupulously refrained from sending its own military personnel into a situation where they might meet their opposite numbers.

Although the Soviet Union loaned some engineering units to the North Vietnamese, they successfully avoided any encounter with American forces. There was no Soviet interference with the Berlin airlift. The U.S. took no direct part in the Afghan resistance to the Soviet invasion, while providing abundant logistical support from across the border. Even greater discretion prevailed when insurgents in Soviet-occupied eastern Europe appealed vainly for U.S. support. The installation of Soviet missiles in Cuba was the only Cold War action that threatened to breach Rule Two. It ended with an ignominious Soviet withdrawal, a great surge in the Soviet production of nuclear missiles and an apparent reinforcement of the nuclear rules.

Careful avoidance prevailed in nearly a hundred armed conflicts — both international and internecine - that raged around the globe between 1949 and 1989. As late as 1987, the U.S. and the Soviet Union were jointly nourishing combat operations in Afghanistan, the Persian Gulf, Lebanon, Ethiopia, Angola, Namibia, Kampuchea, Mozambique, Morocco, Cambodia, Somalia, Chad, the Philippines, Nicaragua, El Salvador, Sri Lanka and Myanmar, all in careful compliance with Rule Two. Many of these deadly quarrels would have occurred without superpower involvement but most of them were sustained and prolonged by the support that both sides received from their superpower sponsors.

The Cold War, in retrospect, was an elaborate charade that defied strategic logic by assuming that war between nuclear states was likely and that the side with more nuclear weapons might claim a meaningful victory after the loss of its cities and most of its people. So the U.S. and the Soviet Union set out to achieve numerical superiority by deploying tens of thousands of nuclear weapons. In the late1980s, just before the collapse of the Soviet Union the United States had thirty-six metropolitan areas with populations over one million. A pair of Soviet Delta III submarines, each with sixteen SNNA missiles carrying seven 200-kiloton warheads with a range of 4000 miles, had the capability to destroy every one of those cities from their patrol station off the Chesapeake Bay. The Soviet Union had only 22 metropolitan areas of a million or more, easy targets for a pair of Ohio Class submarines each carrying sixteen missiles armed with eight 100-kiloton warheads, one firing from a position off the Norwegian coast and the other from the Sea of Okhotsk. This would have taken about 25 megatons out of the U.S. inventory of more than 4000 megatons and made no use of intercontinental missiles, cruise missiles or manned bombers. The Soviet Union, targeting more and larger metropolitan areas, might have needed as much as 50 megatons out of its inventory of 8000.

Not content with their respective oversupplies of strategic nuclear weapons, the U.S. and the Soviet Union produced uncounted thousands of handy tactical weapons, including on the American side, a 60-pound backpack weapon, shells designed for jeep-mounted recoilless rifles, 95 pound and 120 pound artillery shells. The Soviet equivalents included backpack weapons with yields up to 2 kilotons, atomic land mines weighing 200 pounds, anti-aircraft nuclear warheads and 120-pound artillery shells with a 200-mile range.[27]

This was sheer MADness, of course, but it passed for foreign policy and, given the inexorable strategic logic—no nuclear state can attack another nuclear state without inviting unacceptable destruction—the great expansion of the two arsenals did no irretrievable harm, except that now, more than fifteen years after the end of the Cold War, the U.S. still threatens Russia, now a "strategic partner", with thousands of nuclear missiles and is threatened in return.

But perhaps it did do irretrievable harm. The Cold War normalized nuclear weapons so that, for Americans and Russians, the possession of ten thousand warheads seemed to confer some advantage over the possession of five thousand warheads, as if they were machine guns or tanks. The apocalyptic character of nuclear weapons was brushed aside in the course of incorporating them into ground, air and naval forces so that each service could get its fair share.

But although the uniqueness of the new weapons was often ignored in the corridors of power, that uniqueness seems to be responsible for three great non-events that have shaped world history for two generations—the failure of the Cold War to break into a shooting war, the complete absence of accidental nuclear detonations and the non-appearance of nuclear terrorism. Nuclear deterrence, it seems, has been far more effective than either nuclear war planners or anti-nuclear activists ever dreamed.

Chapter Four

Nuclear Strategies

The concept of nuclear deterrence was introduced to the world almost as soon as the atomic bomb itself. Bernard Brodie, a 35 year old political scientist at Yale, published a short paper about "The Atomic Bomb and American Security" on November 1, 1945, less than three months after the bombing of Hiroshima. With uncanny assurance, he described the strategic dilemmas that would confront the United States and other powerful nations far into the future.

Brodie's insights overcame large gaps in his information. He was mistakenly convinced that the bomb was too complex for mass production, that long-range rockets lay far in the future, that the world's uranium reserves were very limited and that the bomb's explosive yield could not be significantly increased. He knew that many experts were sure that no other nation had the economic and engineering resources to build an atomic bomb. Somehow, he overcame this factual confusion, insisting that the development of the bomb had become inevitable as soon as physicists understood the principle of atomic fission and that the American nuclear monopoly would be short-lived. He thought it would probably take the Soviet Union two to five years to develop a bomb; in the event, it was done within that range.

This is one of several places in Brodie's 1945 paper where the adversary is identified as the Soviet Union, even though it was still a U.S. ally at the time. Negotiations for the international control of atomic weapons had just begun. With his usual perspicacity, Brodie assumed that the prospects for international control were dim and that military competition between nuclear-armed nations was inevitable. Whether his enormous influence on subsequent strategizing contributed to that outcome is another question. He correctly identified the Soviet Union, Great Britain and France as having the necessary resources to produce atomic bombs of their own. Since these other governments could not be prevented from developing nuclear weapons, Brodie advocated a policy of complete transparency on nuclear matters to ease the transition to the nuclear era, although he recognized that any nuclear agreement with the Soviets must overcome their resistance to inspection and that negotiations leading up to such an agreement would be more likely to arouse suspicion than to allay it - another prediction that events would promptly confirm.

To the question whether the atomic bomb was a *deterrent* from war, Brodie laid out the basis for what in the fullness of time would become Rule Two (a nuclear state must not attack another nuclear state with its national forces).

> . . . it seems hardly likely, at least as among great powers at some distance from each other, that an attack can be so completely a surprise and so overwhelming as to obviate the opponent's striking back with atomic bombs on a large scale. It would make little difference if one power had more bombs and were better prepared to resist them than the opponent. It would in any case undergo tremendous destruction of life and property. [28]

He concluded that no effective defense against nuclear bombardment would ever be developed. The dispersal of urban population would be excessively expensive and disruptive and could easily be overcome by deploying more bombs. Almost as an afterthought, he introduced the first strike/second strike problem that would obsess generations of military planners:

> . . . the facts of life concerning the United States government under its present constitution make it highly unlikely that if war comes, we will receive the first blow rather than deliver it. Thus, our most urgent military problem is to reorganize ourselves to survive a vastly more destructive "Pearl Harbor" than occurred in 1941.[29]

In 1946, Brodie edited a little volume on *The Absolute Weapon: Atomic Power and World Order,* which included his influential papers on "War in the Atomic Age" and "Implications for Military Policy" together with papers on Soviet-American relations and the possibilities of international control by other authors. Brodie's 1946 papers expanded his 1945 paper—some sections reappear verbatim—but there were important differences. The specifications of the Hiroshima bomb were still unknown to him in 1946 but he thought such bombs were too massive to be used for sabotage and was convinced that future research could not reduce their bulk and weight and significantly increase their explosive yield. So he was visualizing bombs on the scale of Hiroshima when he wrote:

> It is now physically possible for air forces no greater than those existing in the recent war to wipe out all the cities of a great nation in a single day[30]

In the 1946 papers, unlike the 1945 paper, the mass production of great numbers of nuclear weapons is taken for granted, the world's uranium resources of uranium are said to be abundant and deterrence is visualized as a numbers game.

> We cannot, of course, assume that if a race in atomic bombs develops each nation will be content to limit its production after it reaches what it assumes to be the critical level. That would in fact be poor strategy because the actual critical level could never be precisely determined in advance. Moreover, nations will be eager to make whatever political capital (in the narrowest sense of the term) can be made out of superiority in numbers.[31]

Brodie's earlier statement that "It would make little difference if one power had more bombs and were better prepared to resist them than the opponent, "- the strategic principle underlying Rule Two - was actually repeated in one of his 1946 papers. But it was undercut by a new emphasis on second-strike capability.

> Thus the first and most vital step in any American security program for the age of atomic bombs is to take measures to guarantee to ourselves in case of attack the possibility of retaliation in kind. [32]

There was another significant shift between 1945 and 1946. In 1945, Brodie had written:

> Obviously, the relative importance of the army and navy in wartime would be considerably diminished if not eliminated by a device that was capable of producing havoc great enough to effect a decision by itself. [33]

The idea that the usefulness of the armed services had been diminished by the advent of the atomic bomb was vigorously contested by military spokesmen in the months after Hiroshima. They advanced three arguments: (1) that there had never been a new weapon for which man had not devised an effective countermeasure; (2) that the atomic bomb was not significantly more effective than existing weapons and (3) that no foreign power was likely to go nuclear in the foreseeable future. Fleet Admiral Chester Nimitz spoke of "the historical truth that at least up to this time, there has never been a weapon against which man has been unable to devise a counterweapon or a defense." President Truman echoed him in a speech to Congress: "Every new weapon will eventually bring some counterdefense against it." General Arnold, the Air Force commander, reported to the Secretary of War that atomic bombs were only effective when the attacker had air superiority. A certain Major de Seversky insisted in magazine articles and speeches that the Hiroshima bomb would not have damaged the New York financial district more than a large conventional bomb. General Groves, the administrator of the Manhattan Project, was quoted as saying that "the bomb is not a problem for us but for our grandchildren."

These arguments were demonstrably weak but since they were made at the highest levels, they were taken seriously.

In Brodie's 1946 papers, there is no mention of a diminished army. On the contrary, he advocates a buildup of men and equipment for a "military establishment which is expected to fight on after the nation has undergone atomic bomb attack and must be prepared to fight with the men already mobilized and with the equipment already in the arsenals." [34] As to the navy, while sea power will play no great role in nuclear war, the navy will still have vital functions in coastal defense and ocean transport.

Thus, within the first year of the nuclear age, the outlines of the Cold War were already clear to America's pioneer defense intellectual. The adversary would be the Soviet Union; the two sides would arm themselves with thousands of nuclear weapons and also deploy huge conventional forces. Neither side could ever win but both sides could lose. Deterrence, Brodie now seemed to say, might work for a while but then would probably fail.

Nations can still save themselves by their own armed strength from subjugation but not from destruction so colossal as to involve complete ruin.[35]

Brodie died in 1978. His last paper on nuclear strategy was apparently written in that same year.[36] A decade earlier, he hadexpressed his disappointment with the field of strategic studies that he founded, writing about the Vietnam war that:

> When we recall how we discussed methods for demonstrating "our superior resolve: without ever questioning whether we would indeed have or deserve to have superiority in that commodity, we realize how puerile was our whole approach to our art.[37]

In his last paper, he recapitulated the main points he had earlier made about deterrence—the urgent necessity of protecting the retaliatory force, the irrelevance of numerical superiority in warheads or delivery vehicles, the ways in which the bomb would govern the tactics and strategy of a future major war, even if not used. Deterrence, he pointed out, was not new. What was new was the degree to which it was intolerable that it should fail. And he italicized that "*in no case is the fear of the consequences of atomic bomb attack likely to be low.*"[38]

In his later works, Brodie reminded his readers that almost all the basic ideas about nuclear weapons and their use had been produced by civilians working outside the military establishment. The nation's military planners had been the consumers, not the creators, of the strategic ideas produced by the so-called defense intellectuals. And he noted that a strategy that relied exclusively on deterrence would always be "uncongenial" to the military planners.

He described how other defense intellectuals had insisted on American vulnerability to a Soviet first strike and how the subsequent introduction of IBMs and SLBMs and MIRVs had reduced that vulnerability without discouraging the long American effort to achieve strategic superiority. Meanwhile, a loud chorus continued to proclaim America's vulnerability to a Soviet attack. Brodie mentioned the very active Committee on the Present Danger and a magazine article by Major General Keegan entitled "Why the Soviet Union Thinks it Could Fight and Win a Nuclear War."[39] The spokesmen of this movement took exception to the policy of deterring nuclear wars rather than winning them. They proposed to abandon deterrence strategies in favor of war-winning strategies. "But what," asked Brodie, "would these people have us do? Unless we intend to initiate or welcome a nuclear war, our peacetime strategy must necessarily be deterrence."

Next he took on the position advocated by a former secretary of defense, James R. Schlesinger, who advocated a way out of the straight-jacketed posture of nuclear deterrence by preparing, in the event of a nuclear crisis, to use a few strategic nuclear weapons in a first strike, to show "resolve" or to "decapitate" the enemy's top command. People who took this position wanted to enlarge the President's options. Brodie thought it more important to reduce them.

Brodie was the first and the most creative of the civilian strategists who produced the ideas on which American nuclear policies were based but he was by no means alone. Scores of other academic men[40] followed him into the same field and established consultant relationships with the Department of Defense. In time, strategic studies became a recognized academic specialty with its own journals, conferences and technical vocabulary.

This was unprecedented. Strategic planning had long been the exclusive domain of high-ranking military officers like Clausewitz, Jomini, and Douhet. Not since Machiavelli in the sixteenth century had a civilian theorized about the art of war[41] and Machiavelli, though a civilian, was not without military experience, having organized the Florentine militia and commanded troops at the siege of Pisa in 1509.

The typical defense intellectual, as described by one of them:

> . . . was an American; a civilian; basically an 'academic' operating from a university or a well-funded research institute, but moving relatively freely between this base and government; and with a commitment to peace and stability, though a combination of deterrence, arms control, and crisis management.[42]

The role of defense intellectuals was peculiar to the United States. Strategic planning was monopolized by military officers in the Soviet Union and discussions of nuclear policy in Britain, France and China were usually confined to official circles.[43] What brought these American civilians into the picture was the intellectually challenging paradox of nuclear deterrence, whereby the non-use of nuclear weapons depends on a guaranteed willingness to use them. That paradox has its roots in the contradiction between the unsuitability of nuclear explosives for waging war and their extraordinary usefulness for threatening war. It presents a problem whose most rational solution is the unthinkable abolition of nuclear weapons—unthinkable because it would leave the world at the mercy of any weapons that eluded abolition. This web of conundrums was more interesting to scholars than to soldiers and since the U.S. held the initiative in nuclear policy from the beginning, the defense intellectuals flourished in this country as nowhere else.

Nuclear strategy also offered another kind of intellectual challenge— the confrontation with extraordinary numbers. By now, most of us are accustomed to think about numbers that lie far outside the range of traditional human experience. We accept, even if we cannot visualize, the unimaginably large numbers with which contemporary astronomers describe the universe and the unimaginably small numbers involved in nanotechnology. But that was not the case in 1945, when it was first calculated that the energy released by the Hiroshima bomb was equivalent to simultaneous head-on collisions at 60 miles an hour of all the motor vehicles in the United States. Even now, it is difficult for the mind to wrap around that statistic or to come to terms with the additional fact that nuclear bombs with thousands of times the yield of the Hiroshima bomb have been tested. One way to avoid confrontation with these transhuman numbers was to view nuclear bombs as just another type of Air Force ordnance. Another way was to call upon professional scholars to imagine the unimaginable. It was, after all, the scientists in the Manhattan Project who during the run-up to the Trinity test calculated the probability that the blast would ignite the earth's atmosphere. (It turned · out to be small.)

Prominent defense intellectuals were best selling-authors as well as consultants to the armed service and some, like Henry Kissinger and Paul Nitze, eventually held high office and shaped nuclear policy. The positions taken by most of them were compatible with the basic Defense Department view that nuclear wars would be fightable and winnable. Even when the SIOP (Strategic Integrated Operational Plan) of the late 1950s called for the nearly simultaneous detonation of thousands of strategic nuclear weapons over vast areas of the globe, the majority of defense intellectuals were not inclined to accept the claim that resulting changes in the composition of the atmosphere together with the mass destruction of humans and other vertebrates, and unpredictable thermal and radioactive effects, "could lead," as a prominent nuclear abolitionist wrote, "to the extinction of mankind. [44] They were equally unimpressed with the technical possibility that a hydrogen bomb coated with cobalt could be intentionally designed to accomplish that extinction.

Most of the work of the defense intellectuals focused on the nuclear confrontation between the United States and the Soviet Union, and on scenarios of response and counter-response to a Soviet attack on western Europe. The threat of that attack became less plausible with each passing decade but the scenarios continued to be reworked well into the 1980s and even beyond. Today's nuclear force posture is still partly based on those scenarios.

The scenarios could only remain plausible if the Soviet threat remained intact and experts were not lacking to insist that it had. A 1984 book by a prominent defense intellectual told us that:

> The central problem of contemporary Western strategy, as viewed from the vantage point of the early 1980s is that it has neglected to account realistically for the growth in Soviet military power.[45]

In 1987, well into the Gorbachev era, a paper by another hawkish defense intellectual asserted that recent developments in microelectronics and photonics now enabled ground forces to be protected from nuclear attack.

> These technological developments will reinforce the Soviet capacity for active defense of its military forces but also its capacity to conduct a strategy of selective attack, for examples, against the Federal Republic of Germany and the Low Countries or against a weakly armed critical flank of NATO . . .[46]

The author's broader message was that there were all sorts of effective defenses against nuclear weapons. But the hawks were never of one mind. Indeed, the leading defense intellectuals were often likened to the theologians of the late Middle Ages with their apocryphal controversies about how many angels could stand on the head of a pin. There were, after all, only a limited number of possible ways of "thinking about the unthinkable," in Herman Kahn's famous phrase, and the possibilities were further limited by the routine overestimation of Soviet capabilities by the defense intellectuals. The two possibilities most often explored were all-out nuclear wars and limited nuclear wars, further subdivided by whether begun with a Soviet invasion of western Europe, a Soviet first strike, an American first strike, or a third party conflict that drew in the superpowers. An all-out nuclear war could be imagined as beginning with a full-scale attack and ending within days, or as escalating from a limited nuclear war that might or might not represent a prior escalation from a conventional war and might have a duration of months or even years. The scenarios of limited nuclear war included an exchange of single cities, followed by negotiation, or a first strike against nuclear targets that destroyed the adversary's second strike capability, or a mutual restriction to tactical nuclear weapons on designated battlefields, or a precise decapitation of the opposing government. The scenarios of all-out nuclear war involved two alternative strategies—an exchange of "counterforce" attacks, directed by each side against the other's nuclear arsenal, or an exchange of "countervalue" attacks intended to destroy the adversary's cities and kill as many of its people as possible. American official policy oscillated between these alternatives, although counterforce targeting became indistinguishable from counter value targeting at some level of intensity.

The details of the bitter disputes among defense intellectuals and their clients in government and the military establishment are too complex to be fully described here. An admirable account covering the first forty years of the nuclear age can be found in Gregg Herken's *Counsels of War.*[47] What matters for our present purposes is that each individual dispute arose from one or another of the dilemmas that blocked the quest for a winning nuclear strategy. The earliest and most persistent of these dilemmas was the choice between total and limited nuclear war. While one set of strategists argued that no government would start a nuclear war knowing that it would be a total war and equivalent to national suicide for the parties, another set insisted on the possibility of a limited nuclear war that would never escalate to total war. It was claimed that this could be accomplished by using only tactical nuclear weapons, or by using them only to decapitate the hostile government, or by "intrawar signaling" that nuclear attacks would be limited to specified targets

As we have seen, Eisenhower alternated between the limited war position and the total war position during his eight years in office. Kennedy moved from the total war to the limited war position in his shorter time. Henry Kissinger made his initial reputation by a carefully reasoned argument for limited war.[8] Herman Kahn tried to straddle the issue with a ladder of graduated nuclear choices.[49]

On the limited war side, there was a subsidiary division between the advocates of counterforce targeting (military assets) and countervalue targeting (cities and civilian populations). As nuclear arsenals grew in size and yield, the distinction became somewhat academic, since so many military installations were located in cities—there were said to be 170 military targets in Moscow alone.[50] Yet in the 1970s, when the advent of MIRVs made silo-based missiles theoretically vulnerable, countervalue strategies enjoyed a brief vogue.

There was also a subsidiary division on the total war side between the strategists who maintained that a total nuclear war could be won in some meaningful sense (although badly damaged, the U.S. would "prevail") and those who insisted that a total nuclear war could have no winner. That question is still unresolved.

Another intensely debated issue was whether the U.S. should plan for a first strike or a second strike. The majority adhered to a scenario in which a nuclear first strike would be launched by the Soviet Union either out of the blue or as a consequence of an ongoing conventional war in Europe, with the object of destroying the U.S. capacity for a second strike response. The seemingly senseless growth of the U.S. nuclear arsenal in the 1950s was rooted in the perceived necessity of maintaining a second strike capability to destroy the Soviet Union after absorbing a first strike whose precise scale could not be accurately predicted. But there was always an influential body of opinion, especially in the Pentagon, that preferred to visualize an American first strike, either out of the blue at a moment of opportunity, or to rescue a failing ground campaign. The U.S. has never adopted a policy of no-first use although often urged to do so.[51]

The most contentious controversy - still active today—raged over ABM systems, first proposed in the 1950s, then partly banned by the1972 Anti- Ballistic Missile Treaty with the Soviet Union that allowed only two local missile defense systems (later reduced to one) on either side. The announced intention of the treaty was to preserve symmetrical vulnerability—an idea especially repugnant to many of the nuclear hawks. The United States repudiated the treaty in 2002 and set about installing some elements of a continental missile defense system, although after fifty years of intense debate and costly research, an effective anti-ballistic system is still not in sight and it seems likely that if such a system were ever developed, it could be bypassed with relative ease by other delivery vehicles.

Another question that aroused strong feelings and mobilized opposing factions for many years was whether the goal of U.S. nuclear policy

ought to be parity or superiority. The collapse of the Soviet Union
seemed to assure U.S. superiority but the question was revived in 2003
by the bilateral Treaty of Moscow, which seemed to mandate nuclear
parity between the parties.

Of course there were doves among the defense intellectuals [52] who
advocated the drastic reduction and even the abolition of nuclear arsenals or who pursued Brodie's and Oppenheimer's old idea of substituting complete transparency for the secrecy and security surrounding nuclear weapons, but since their views were generally "uncongenial" to
military planners, they had little access to classified information and
negligible influence on strategic planning.

After September 11, 2001, official American policy shifted to an emphasis on preemption and the "war on terrorism" so that nuclear deterrence seemed to go out of style—at least officially. A paper on deterrence by Colin Gray that appeared in 2003 under the aegis of the Army
War College attempted to strike a new balance between deterrence and
preemption and explored the possible deterrence of terrorists.

> The facts that many individual members of al Qaeda would welcome mar-
> tyrdom and that the organization has nonnegotiable goals are really beside
> the point. Of course, al Qaeda cannot be deterred by the possible death of
> some of its troops; the blood of martyrs will attract new recruits. How-
> ever, the organization itself, in loose-knit sophisticated network form
> though it is, should be eminently deterrrable.

Gray, however, did not draw a sharp line between nuclear deterrence
and deterrence by other means.

An option seldom if ever explored by defense intellectuals or military
planners was the possibility of a durable armed truce between hostile
nuclear-weapons states—the only nuclear scenario that has so far
played out in the real world.

Chapter Five

Non-Events

Besides the remarkable absence of active hostilities in the Cold War, there were two other non-events that loomed large in the military history of the past sixty years. Neither was predicted and even in retrospect, they seem improbable. But here they are, and anyone trying to understand the contemporary war system must come to terms with them.

No nuclear weapon has ever been detonated by accident.
No nuclear weapon has ever been deployed other than by than a national government.

Either record might be broken overnight, but even in retrospect, these twin sixty-year records would be remarkable.

All high-powered machinery is expected to cause occasional accidents and a small branch of social science has sprung up to interpret "normal accidents" and calculate risk-benefit ratios.

The theory of normal accidents is succinctly explained by Charles Perrow, who coined the term. In relation to high-risk technologies he proposes that:

> . . . no matter how effective conventional safety devices are, there is a form of accident that is inevitable. This is not good news for systems that have high catastrophic potential, such as nuclear power plants, nuclear weapons systems, recombinant DNA production, or even ships carrying highly toxic or explosive cargoes.[53]

He goes on to explain that special features of high-risk systems like these that make accidents in them normal. Such systems have many interacting components that are individually subject to failure. It is inevitable, according to Perrow, that concurrent failures in two or more components will interact in some unexpected way to cause the entire system to fail.

He proves the point by reviewing the history of normal (and catastrophic) accidents in nuclear power plants, petrochemical plants, aircraft and airways, marine traffic, space travel and other high-risk systems. He devotes considerable space to the fictional catastrophe in Kubrick's *Dr. Strangelove* and even more space to the weaknesses of America's early warning system against nuclear attack but then acknowledges that in this particular case, the "inevitable" catastrophe has somehow been avoided.

American nuclear weapons have been involved in hundreds of accidents.[54] They have been jettisoned over water and over land. Planes loaded with live bombs have crashed, collided on the ground, collided in the air, burned, exploded, and broken up in mid-air. One submarine carrying nuclear missiles was lost at sea. Weapons have been smashed, incinerated, flooded, and dropped from heights. Missiles in silos have burned and exploded. Foreign, especially Soviet and Russian, nuclear forces are known to have suffered similar accidents.

Some of the nuclear weapons involved in these accidents were destroyed by fire, others by detonation of their explosive triggers. Some broke apart and scattered radioactivity over a local area. Some were lost and never found. In not a single case did the nuclear core explode.

In principle, accidental detonation might occur by human failure, such as the unauthorized launching of a nuclear weapon against a potential adversary by a rogue submarine captain and his compliant officers. Or it might be due to mechanical failure. When Warren Air Force Base in Cheyenne, Wyoming, recorded a message in January 1984 that one of its Minuteman III ballistic missiles was about to launch from its silo due to a computer malfunction, an armored car was parked on the lid of the silo to keep it closed.

A number of false alarms about hostile incoming missiles are known to have brought U.S. forces to the brink of a nuclear response. Each incident failed safe. The details are mostly classified except for the brief period between October 1979 and June 1980, when no less that four threat assessment conferences were convened for what turned out to be false alarms—a falling piece of an old rocket that was mistakenly identified as an incoming submarine-launched missile, a training tape with a simulation of a Soviet attack that was accidentally fed into a NORAD computer, a stray Soviet intermediate-range missile that appeared to be heading towards the United States, and a faulty computer chip that caused display screens to show a massive Soviet attack.[55] In the training tape incident, computers at three military command centers all showed that the Soviet Union had launched more than 200 missiles in the direction of the United States.

False alarms have been equally common on the other side; the most dramatic occurred in 1995 when Russian radar operators discovered that a rocket fired from the Norwegian coast was headed in their direction. While President Yeltsin and his advisers prepared a nuclear response, the object was found to be a Norwegian weather rocket. An advance notice of its launch had gone astray in Russian channels.[56]

It is obvious that tens of thousands of obscure soldiers and civilians in this and other countries have taken extraordinary care to prevent an accidental nuclear detonation—much greater care than is taken in any other situation involving human agents and complex mechanical systems.

A book by John McPhee that appeared more than thirty years ago under the curious title of *The Curve of Binding Energy*[57] reported McPhee's running interview over many months with Ted Taylor, the scientist-engineer who designed many of America's most ingenious nuclear weapons, including the miniaturized models most suitable for terrorist use. The two men explored several related questions. How many unauthorized amateurs would it take to build a bomb in the kiloton range? How would they obtain the fissile material? Where would they get the technical specifications?

Taylor acknowledged that opinions differed on the first point but he thought that a single technically competent individual might be able to build a bomb alone. Finding the fissile material should not be a problem in a world awash with the plutonium produced as a byproduct of nuclear energy production and with quantities of enriched uranium shipped by commercial carriers every day. The essential technical information was already available in unclassified official documents together with recipes for converting these materials into explosive cores.

He must have known of, but did not mention, an experiment conducted by the United States government a few years earlier to find out
what it would take to develop a viable fission weapon starting from
scratch. In that experiment, which ran from 1963 to 1967, three newly
graduated physics students were asked to design a workable nuclear
weapon using information in the public domain. They succeeded after
three man-years of collective effort.[58] Nevertheless, Taylor doubted that
terrorists would take that path.

> But why go on to steal, say, uranium hexafluoride and convert it to metal
> and fabricate a crude weapon when the military has tens of thousands of
> extremely well-made bombs distributed all over the world? . . . why
> bother?—in the light of the more straightforward alternative of stealing a
> bomb.[59]

Taylor envisaged a terrorist attack on Manhattan centered on the World
Trade Center long before the idea occurred to certain jihadists, but Taylor expected the attack to be carried out with a portable nuclear weapon.

> Through free air, a kiloton bomb will send a lethal dose of immediate ra-
> diation up to half a mile. Anyone in an office facing the Trade Center
> would die. People in that building over there would get them first. Next
> comes visible light. Next the neutrons. Then the air shock. Then missiles.
> Unvaporized concrete would go out of here at the speed of a rifle shot. A
> steel-and-concrete missile flux would go out one mile and would include
> in all maybe a tenth of the weight of the building: about five thousand
> tons.[60]

The actual attack at the very same place on September 11, 2001, using
two airliners as guided missiles, took 3025 lives. Had al Qaeda used
Taylor's simpler method, the death toll would have been very much
greater. The Saudis and Egyptians who planned the World Trade Center
attack were technically sophisticated and might well have turned their
ingenuity to the theft of a Russian backpack nuclear weapon or even to
the construction of a home-made device, using stolen or purchased fissile material. Sinister events of that kind are visualized every day in security protocols and emergency plans.

Hundreds of books and articles have told the same story—it should
be relatively easy for terrorists to build a simple nuclear bomb and even
easier to steal one from the vast and ill-guarded Russian inventory.

Cote's authoritative 1996 primer on fissile materials and nuclear weapon design lays out the mind-boggling complexity of advanced weapons engineering—tritium boosting, mixed fuels, beryllium reflectors, sealed pits and so forth—but reiterates that none of these refinements are essential.

> Thus we see that there are very simple nuclear weapon designs available to potential proliferators. Weapons based on these designs would bear little resemblance to the more advanced weapons deployed by today's nuclear powers, but that is beside the point, since even simple weapons could reliably produce an explosion equal to hundreds or thousands of tons of TNT. That is a much easier task than most people think; the main obstacle has been the difficulty of securing an adequate supply of fissile material.[61]

Other reliable sources tell us that some Russian warehouses holding fissile materials are protected only by a simple padlock, that quantities of weapons-grade uranium and plutonium have gone missing even in the U.S., that fissile materials could probably be bought from Pakistan or North Korea. A report on the Kurchatov Institute, nine miles from the Kremlin, improved with U.S. funding and considered Russia's most secure facility, mentions a building that holds enough highly-enriched uranium for half a dozen large warheads but lacks an alarm system or a secure fence.[62]

A 2004 book on nuclear terrorism by Graham Allison[63] presents a more recent version of this theme. He tells us that thousands of weapons and tens of thousands of uranium and plutonium cores are stored in unsecured locations in Russia and hundreds of confirmed thefts have occurred at these sites since the collapse of the Soviet Union. Like Ted Taylor thirty-two years earlier, Allison thought it would not be particularly difficult for moderately skilled terrorists to build a basic atomic bomb in which a slug of highly enriched uranium is fired down a gun barrel into a hollowed target of the same material to form a supercritical mass and explode. With a hundred pounds of fissile material, the explosive yield should be in the range of the Hiroshima bomb. But like Taylor, Allison said it would be more convenient for terrorists to steal a bomb than to make one. The Soviet Union produced thousands of tactical nuclear weapons of various types, some weighing as little as 65 pounds, others a little heavier, but all light enough and small enough to fit into the trunk of a passenger car. Many of them are still around. Their yields range from a fraction of a kiloton to 2 kilotons, but even a 0.5 kiloton bomb would have an explosive yield equal to 200 of the largest conventional bombs in the U.S. arsenal. As usual, superlatives falter in the presence of nuclear numbers. Allison asks us to visualize the Hiroshima bomb converted to sticks of dynamite packed tightly in a column one-foot square and two and a half miles high.

But why stop at the kiloton level? The Russian storehouse includes individual thermonuclear bombs with more power than all the explosive weapons used in all the wars since the invention of gunpowder. Some of these weigh as little as 800 pounds and could be carried in the back of a pickup truck.

Allison has something more to add to his readers' sleepless nights:

> Concern about a nuclear terrorist attack on the capital led to the construction in November 2001 of . . . a grid of hundreds of sophisticated radiation detection devices at major points of approach to the nation's capital . . . Aircraft and ground vehicles also patrolled the city with mobile sensors. According to Bush administration officials, during large-scale operational trials the sensors repeatedly failed to identify threatening radioactive signatures.[64]

The nuclear rules do not prohibit the use of nuclear weapons by non-governmental groups against either nuclear or non-nuclear states. A nuclear attack by Islamic jihadists is generally agreed to be the most serious threat the United States faces today and one for which the country is not adequately prepared.

The continued worldwide non-occurrence of a nuclear terrorist event is a puzzle as well as a blessing. If as so many experts have testified so often, it would not be excessively difficult for terrorists to obtain and use a nuclear weapon, why they have not done it?[65] The simplest explanation might be that al Qaeda and other currently active terrorist groups lack the technical facilities to work with nuclear materials. Considered as a tactical operation—without reference to the boundless malice that inspired it—the September 11 attack was a model of minimalist design. The men who planned it in Hamburg were technically trained but lacked a technical support structure. Hence, their ingenious use of available resources—flight training, airline tickets, box-cutters and their willingness to die—to achieve spectacular results. Happily for us, their demise in the operation seems to have left al Qaeda without the immediate capability for anything more sophisticated than the conventional explosives on which their other operations have relied.

A more speculative explanation is that nuclear deterrence works even for hardened terrorists. The outsize effects of nuclear weapons may inspire enough deep-seated fear to discourage them from going that route, while at the same time, a concern about nuclear reprisal might be especially acute among jihadists who see the United States and other western nations as totally evil and therefore capable of all the atrocities that nuclear weapons make possible — such as the obliteration of Mecca and Medina.

I am not entirely convinced by this line of reasoning but the facts speak for themselves -

sixty years and counting without a single verified attempt at a nuclear terrorist attack. Of the ten terrorist plots described by the White House as foiled by U.S. and allied intelligence agencies between September 2001 and October 2005, none had anything to do with nuclear weapons.[66]

It would be foolish, of course, to ignore the danger of nuclear terrorism. The damage inflicted on the American way of life by the September 11 hijackers went far beyond the death and destruction at the World Trade Center and the Pentagon, and it reopened one of the questions explored by McPhee and Taylor long ago. What fraction of a modern society needs to be knocked out to make it collapse?

That question raises its ugly head every time we board an airliner and are elaborately searched to prevent a repetition of the September 11 action, although we know such an event is highly improbable. The passengers on three of the four planes hijacked on that tragic day were not aware of their intended fate and allowed themselves to be subdued by a few lightly armed men. As soon as the passengers on the fourth plane learned by cell phone what was in store for them, they rose up and stormed the hijackers, aborting the terrorist strike. The passengers in any future hijacking would presumably do the same, with or without the federal marshals who might be traveling along. Even if they did not, the barricading of cockpit doors has made hijacking impractical.[67]

We can hardly begin to imagine the restrictions on personal freedom that would follow an act of nuclear terrorism. But there is at least a chance that nuclear terrorism will continue to be deterred. In other respects, the strategic situation of the United States continues to be more favorable than anyone in Washington seems to recognize. The probability of an attack on this country by the armed forces of a foreign government is close to zero and likely to remain so for the foreseeable future.

A July 2005 editorial in the New York Times argued for expanding the Army by 100,000 new solders and paying for them by shrinking the Navy and the Air Force. The editorial went on, in cheerful ignorance of the nuclear rules, to list possible contingencies for an enlarged U.S. Army to meet over the new few years—a Chinese attack on Taiwan, a North Korean attack on South Korea or Japan, a takeover of Saudi Arabia by al Qaeda, a terrorist coup in Pakistan, together with continuing operations in Iraq and Afghanistan.

The empty thinking behind this list assumed that American troops might be sent to fight the Chinese in Taiwan, the North Koreans in South Korea, an al Qaeda regime in Saudi Arabia or a rogue regime in Pakistan. The U.S. is imagined as attacking unfriendly regimes in Pakistan and North Korea, with no awareness of Rule Two, which prohibits a nuclear-weapons state from attacking another nuclear-weapons state. A U.S. attack on Saudi Arabia after a hypothetical al Qaeda takeover would not violate any of the nuclear rules, but with the experience of Iraq in the background, who can seriously contemplate putting American boots on the ground in an invasion of Saudi Arabia?

Every contemporary war game of this kind points to the same conclusion. There are no imaginable major operations for U.S. ground forces that make strategic sense. Imagining them in public, however, is not a cost-free exercise. It encourages China, North Korea, Pakistan and Iran—the latter not mentioned by the *Times*—to develop their nuclear assets in order to bask more comfortably in the protection offered by Rule Two. That expansion may not even be necessary. As the timorous six-party negotiations with North Korea show so clearly, a nation does not need much of a nuclear arsenal to enjoy immunity from attack by the armed forces of other nations.

Yet in the spring of 2006, the Bush administration was openly considering a war with Iran, and having insufficient available troops for a ground offensive, was announcing plans for a large-scale air attack on Iran with the nuclear option "on the table."[68] The proposed attack was intended to prevent Iran from acquiring nuclear weapons and also to achieve regime change in that country. As in the case of Iraq, there were no publicized plans for dealing with post-attack conditions.

The U.S., with more nuclear weapons than can ever be used and the means of delivering them anywhere in the world, need not fear armed attack by any foreign nation. We can and should fear nuclear terrorism but recognize that it may never occur.

Chapter Six

The Nuclear Taboo

According to Rule Three, "A nuclear state may attack a non-nuclear state with its national forces, if the attacked state has no nuclear guarantor."

The invasion and occupation of Iraq by the U.S. and Britain in 2003 were actions in conformity with Rule Three. So was the Gulf War of 1991, the Falklands War between Britain and Argentina, the invasion of Lebanon by Israel, the Chinese seizure of Tibet, the U.S. actions in Korea and Vietnam, and the Soviet invasion of Afghanistan. But note the failure of the Anglo-French attempt on the Suez Canal in 1956, to which the U.S. and the Soviet Union responded as nuclear guarantors for Egypt. Note too the continuing reluctance of China to take military action against Taiwan, with the U.S. as the island's nuclear guarantor.

But Rule Three seems to be silent on whether a nuclear state may use nuclear weapons in its war against a non-nuclear state. Such use has often been considered and as often rejected. It seems to be subject to a taboo against the first use of nuclear weapons that developed gradually during the Cold War.

The first reaction of the federal government after the Soviet Union tested its first atom bomb in 1949 was to preach the urgent necessity of civil defense. Citizens were urged to build backyard shelters, and there was a lively debate in the media about whether it was legitimate for shelter occupants to shoot intrusive neighbors who had not built shelters of their own. Children were taught to crouch under their school desks with their heads on their knees during a nuclear alert. Every sizeable community developed a network of communal shelters stocked with emergency rations and medical supplies and an underground command center to shelter local officials and their families. Evacuation routes were mapped of every large city. The Army began to divide its infantry divisions into "pentomic" units for easy dispersal. More than a million people offered themselves as volunteers to the new Civil Defense Administration in 1951, including ten thousand New York City taxi drivers who volunteered to assist evacuation in case of a nuclear alert. The enthusiasm was short-lived. The principal accomplishment of the CDA was to build a mock American city in the Nevada desert and blow it to pieces with a middle-size atomic bomb. It also staged a number of unsuccessful evacuation drills, in consequence of which the need for high-capacity evacuation routes became a major selling point for the Interstate Highway System.

Interest in civil defense revived with the Kennedy administration. As relations with the Soviet Union deteriorated over the building of the Berlin Wall, Washington announced plans for constructing or improvising fallout shelters for the entire U.S. population. The plans were quickly forgotten after the Cuban missile crisis and the advent of serious arms control negotiations with the Soviets.

The third, and so far the last wave of interest in civil defense spanned the years from 1974 to 1981. It took the form of Crisis Relocation Planning, which envisaged the temporary evacuation of 400 high-risk areas in case of a nuclear alert.[69] The Federal Emergency Management Agency, which had a respectable reputation at that time, claimed that the program would save 80 or 85 million lives in an all-out nuclear attack. Crisis relocation was planned to be short-term—for no more than fourteen days - and voluntary - it was estimated that 10 to 20 percent of those called on to evacuate would refuse to leave their homes. The federal government would provide evacuees with food, fuel and facilities. Special arrangements would be made for relocating government officials at all levels, beginning with the President and his sixteen constitutionally designated successors.

There were two diametrically opposed theories about the probable effect of crisis relocation in an actual crisis. The official theory was that it would discourage a Soviet attack by (a) showing resolve and (b) decreasing the number of American casualties. The contrary view was that the mass evacuation of cities would signal that the U.S. was preparing a nuclear strike and give the Soviets a strong incentive to strike first. Over time, the contrary view prevailed, together with greater realism about the logistics of evacuating major metropolitan areas and the realization that it might be impossible to restrict relocation to a maximum of fourteen days. So the plans for crisis relocation were quietly shelved, except those for relocating office-holders, which expanded over the years.[70]

After the collapse of the Soviet Union, interest in civil defense for the general population reached a new low; FEMA was systematically underfunded and eventually ousted from the Cabinet. The day of reckoning for the agency arrived with Hurricane Katrina.

While the American public was only intermittently concerned about the threat of nuclear war, the government's long, arduous search for a war-fighting doctrine that would permit the use of nuclear weapons continued without interruption. From the outset, it was clear to the defense intellectuals and their military counterparts that the side making a first nuclear strike would have an enormous advantage, particularly if that strike were concentrated on the planes and missiles of the other side. The toughest-minded did not hesitate to urge a pre-emptive nuclear attack on the Soviet Union, but without reliable information about Soviet capabilities, they could not be sure about the retaliatory consequences. The less tough-minded, examining the other side of the coin, assumed that the Soviet Union, being more evil than the U.S., would be likely to launch a first strike with less concern for the consequences. They placed enormous importance on the development of a second-strike capability.

The Korean War was the first major conflict after World War II that seemed to invite the use of atomic weapons. When American and South Korean troops fighting under the banner of the United Nations approached the northern border of North Korea in November 1950 and were on the verge of victory, they were driven back by a massive wave of Chinese "volunteers."

At a news conference soon after, President Truman said he would take whatever steps were necessary to meet the military situation and when asked whether that would include the use of atomic bombs, the President said that it would and that General MacArthur would decide whether and when to use them. As opposition built, the statement was retracted and the President gave assurances that there was no immediate intention of using atomic weapons in Korea and that the decision to do so would be reserved to himself as commander-in-chief. It was MacArthur's public disagreement with this revised policy that led Truman to dismiss him from command. There was no further consideration of using atomic weapons in Korea until January 1953 when, Eisenhower, who had campaigned for the presidency on a promise to end the war quickly, ordered the Air Force to develop a plan for ending it with atomic weapons.[71] That plan, which included the nuclear bombardment of Chinese airfields was quietly shelved, apparently for fear of Soviet retaliation, but three years later, with Korea much in mind, Secretary of State Dulles unveiled the policy of "massive retaliation." The gist of it was that if the communists broke the cease fire in Korea, the U.S. response would not necessarily be confined to Korea. The threat was clearly nuclear. Other nuclear threats by the Eisenhower administration were directed against the People's Republic of China during the Taiwan Strait crises of 1954-55 and 1958, and seem to have been moderately effective. It is not clear at this distance of time whether the intermediate-range nuclear weapons the U.S. loaned to Chiang Kai-Shek to defend against a possible Chinese invasion of Taiwan remained under U.S. control or what ultimately became of them.

The 1950s also saw attempts to imagine limited nuclear war, either by downsizing nuclear weapons or by restricting them to genuine military targets. It was never clear why belligerents capable of making and keeping such fine-tuned agreements would want to assume the apocalyptic risks of nuclear war. It was equally unclear how the military targets located in and near population centers could be separated from their surroundings in a nuclear blast.

As the U.S. Soviet confrontation intensified in the early 1960s, each side consistently misjudged the other's preparations and intentions. Kennedy, campaigning in 1960, promised to close a nonexistent missile gap. Khrushchev, soon after, seemed to be compensating for a real missile gap, by emplacing medium-range missiles in Cuba. But recent research suggests that Khrushchev was more concerned with protecting Cuba's communist regime—the only one ever established outside of the immediate Soviet orbit—from a U.S. invasion than with correcting the balance of nuclear power. In that respect, he was successful, since the crisis elicited an American pledge to abstain from further incursions in Cuba. But it also demonstrated the strategic inferiority of the Soviet Union, which thereupon began a successful effort to overtake the United States in missiles and warheads.

The Cuban missile crisis had another effect. It frightened the leaders who experienced it with the realization that their existing nuclear arsenals presented an intolerable threat to both sides. The era of arms control agreements began almost overnight.

The invention of MIRVs (multiple independently targeted re-entry vehicles) with a number of separately targeted warheads mounted on a single missile, gave the U.S. the assured ability to destroy every Russian population center several times over in "surgical strikes" and conferred a brief advantage until the Soviets developed MIRVs of their own. The U.S. then attempted to protect its own missiles from Soviet surgical strikes by elaborate measures for dispersal and concealment. Meanwhile, the development by both sides of essentially invulnerable SLBMs (submarine launched ballistic missiles) made all other means of warhead delivery superfluous and gave each side an unchallengeable second-strike capability. Bureaucratic inertia preserved land-based ballistic missiles, cruise missiles, artillery shells and long-range bombers as nuclear vehicles, but they became almost irrelevant to the superpower confrontation.

During the Kennedy administration, Secretary of Defense McNamara initially proposed a subtle countervalue strategy whereby the U.S. would attack Soviet cities but refrain from attacking military targets. Then, a B-52 carrying two twenty-four megaton hydrogen bombs disintegrated over North Carolina. Five crew members and one of the gigantic bombs parachuted to the ground, the other bomb crashed and broke apart without detonating. All but one of its safety devices failed, however. A little later, a false alarm at NORAD indicated that a massive Soviet missile attack was under way. Soon after, McNamara was briefed on the SIOP inherited from the Eisenhower administration which called for the destruction of nearly all the cities and towns of the Soviet Union as well as targets in China and eastern Europe, with a projected loss of more than 300 million lives, The shock of these successive events persuaded McNamara that even if a nuclear bomb fell on the U.S., a nuclear response should be withheld until the damage had been assessed and communication with Soviet leaders had been established..

Another attempt to find a formula for nuclear war began in the 1950s with a plan for a continental system of ballistic missile defense, later revived as Nixon's Strategic Defense Initiative, then renewed again as Reagan's Star Wars project, and resuscitated once more as Bush's National Missile Defense Initiative, all of which undertook the apparently impossible task of developing a perfect defense against land-based intercontinental missiles, without providing any defense at all against other delivery vehicles.

Outside of the U.S.-Soviet confrontation, the effort to find a military use for nuclear weapons continued. The nuclear bombing of Hanoi was repeatedly proposed during the Vietnam War, but foundered on the possibility of Soviet or Chinese retaliation. With the passage of time, it became clear that the use of nuclear force by a nuclear state against a non-nuclear state would be hazardous to the user, because the consequences of breaking the nuclear taboo were unpredictable.

The taboo was not planned. It grew out of the failure of decision-makers to find a practical military use for nuclear weapons after 1945 together with the first-strike/second-strike scenarios, which took for granted that any attack on a nuclear state by national forces would provoke a nuclear response. Indeed, during the Cold War, systems were in place to make that response automatic. Similar systems to assure a nuclear response to a nuclear attack on the U.S. are in place today and could allegedly be triggered by the mere warning of an impending attack. In one view, "the President's supporting command system isn't actually geared to withhold retaliation in the event of an enemy missile attack, real or apparent."[72]

The rejection of innumerable proposals by senior U.S. officials for the first use of nuclear weapons during the past sixty years and the unbroken nuclear abstinence of other nuclear powers have created a strong taboo against first use. As with taboos in more primitive societies, there seems to be a deep-seated fear that a violation of that taboo would plunge the social order—in this case, the international system—into chaos. The taboo does not provide total protection, but the longer it remains unbroken the stronger it gets.

The Bush administration's effort to undercut the nuclear taboo began with the Pentagon's *Nuclear Posture Review* dated January 8, 2002.[73] Its connection with the September 11 attack is difficult to discern but its tone was new and sharp. The U.S. had never committed itself to a policy of no-first-use of nuclear weapons but neither had it ever embraced a contrary policy. This document announced an intention to use nuclear weapons both offensively and defensively whenever convenient. Immediate contingencies for the application of nuclear force were identified as an Iraqi attack on Israel or its neighbors, a North Korean attack on South Korea, a military confrontation with China over the status of Taiwan. Remoter contingencies were mentioned in connection with Syria, Iran, Libya, China (aside from Taiwan) and Russia. The extraordinary frankness of this unclassified document was obviously intended to signal a change in long-standing U.S. policy. A more elaborate version of the new approach to nuclear strategy was the *Doctrine for Joint Nuclear Operations,* also unclassified, issued by the Pentagon in March 2005.[74] Section III of that document laid out the purposes for which theater commanders might request presidential approval for the employment of nuclear weapons. They were broad enough to cover almost any type of combat operation. Nuclear weapons might be used against "an adversary using or intending to use WMD against U.S., multinational or alliance forces" or for attacks against "deep hardened bunkers containing chemical or biological weapons or the C2 [command and control] infrastructure required for the adversary to execute a WMD attack against the United States or its friends and allies" and " to counter potentially overwhelming adversary conventional forces" and "for rapid and favorable war termination on U.S. terms" and "to ensure success of U.S. and multinational operations" and "to demonstrate U.S. intent and capability to use nuclear weapons to deter adversary use of WMD" and "to respond to adversary-supplied WMD use by surrogates against U.S. and multinational forces or civilian populations." This last item was a discreet reference to the nuclear targeting of sub-national groups.

Another striking feature of the new doctrine was the assertion that the United States would not be deterred in any way by weapons of mass destruction in the hands of potential adversaries. Rule Two was to be discarded along with the nuclear taboo

The most extraordinary aspect of this important initiative was how little public attention it received when it was announced in March 2005. Not until six months later did the *New York Times* report that, "The Pentagon is preparing new guidelines governing the use of nuclear weapons that foresee possible pre-emptive strikes against terrorist groups or nations planning to use unconventional weapons against the United States."[75]

At first, only the physicists, reminded once more of their historic role in weapons development, reacted. Within a month, 470 American physicists, including seven Nobel laureates, had signed a petition protesting the new doctrine. According to the scientists:

> This dangerous policy ignores the fact that nuclear weapons are on a completely different scale than other WMDs and conventional weapons. Using a nuclear weapon pre-emptively and against a non-nuclear adversary crosses a line, blurring the sharp distinction between nuclear and non-nuclear weapons and heightens the probability of future use by others.

That didn't get much publicity either. Nevertheless, once the news was out, opposition began to build in Congress, in the press, and within the armed services. On February 2, 2006, the Pentagon formally canceled the entire Doctrine. The challenge to the nuclear taboo seemed to be withdrawn.

Then, a few weeks later, the Pentagon leaked its operational plans for an air attack on Iran, designed to put a final stop to that country's nuclear ambitions. The details were spelled out in a long *New Yorker* article by Seymour Hersh[76] whose reports on the government's military activities are regarded as semi-official. According to Hersh, one of the plans for a regime-changing operation in Iran that was presented to the White House, called for using bunker-buster tactical nuclear weapons against underground Iranian sites. But although the plan originated in the Pentagon, it aroused misgivings there. At one point, Hersh reports, the Joint Chiefs of Staff sought to remove the nuclear option from the evolving war plans and were rebuffed. "The bottom line," said an unnamed Pentagon source, "is that Iran cannot become a nuclear-weapons state. The problem is that the Iranians realize that only by becoming a nuclear state can they defend themselves against the U.S. Something bad is going to happen." [77]

Almost at the same time, under the heading "War Plans for Iran Are an Open Secret" the *Washington Post* provided additional information about operation TIRANNT (theater Iran near term) under which Army and U.S. Central Command planners have been examining scenarios for war with Iran. [78] As part of this open secret, Secretary Rumsfeld had alerted the U.S. Strategic Command in Omaha to prepare to implement a strike plan that included Iran. The task force charged with this effort was reported to "worry" that if it were called upon to deliver prompt strikes against certain targets in Iran under certain circumstances, the President might have to be told that the only option was a nuclear one.

Another article by Hersh, in the summer of 2006, described continued Pentagon resistance to either conventional or nuclear bombing of Iran.[79]

What can be read from these open secrets is that the Bush administration has considered an attack on Iran to put a stop to its nuclear programs and change its regime. What cannot be read is whether that operation would include the first belligerent use of nuclear weapons since 1945. As this is written, negotiations with Iran are proceeding and the nuclear taboo remains unbroken.

The taboo is continually fortified by the practical arrangements that government agencies and business corporations take to prepare for "the day after World War III."[80]

In March 2006, it was revealed that since 9/11 the U.S. has had a shadow government, in which about 100 senior civilian managers live and work secretly in fortified and undisclosed locations outside Washington.[81] It has long been known that whenever the President and his sixteen designated successors might appear together—as at a State of the Union address—at least one of the successors is invariably absent, ready to take over if all the others are killed by a nuclear strike. Less important government posts have equally long succession ladders. The same source recently reported that a new order of succession had been established for the directorship of the National Archives and Record Administration, detailing the order of succession to the directorship down to the tenth level.

The details of doomsday scenarios have naturally varied over time. In the most popular fictional account—Nevil Shute's *On the Beach*, published in 1957 - the last humans are attractive young naval families trying to live normal lives in an Australian town while waiting to be extinguished by the drifting radioactivity released by a nuclear war in the northern hemisphere. Critics soon pointed out that global air currents follow a different path but the plausibility of human extinction as an unintended consequence of nuclear war was not seriously questioned.

As previously noted, the project of evacuating major metropolitan areas in a nuclear crisis was abandoned many years ago, but elaborate doomsday accommodations for officials and (usually) their families have been a standard feature of the nuclear age, both for public officials and for the top managers of business corporations and eleemosynary institutions. In the heyday of FEMA, in the early 1980s, nearly every American community larger than a village, had installed an emergency command center—usually underground, with blast protection, filtered air, and large supplies of food and water—to house local officials deemed sufficiently important to be protected in case of a nuclear alert or comparable emergency, together with their immediate families. The existence of these facilities was generally unknown to ordinary citizens.[82]

The national government, of course, did things on a much larger scale. At the Greenbrier Hotel in the mountains of West Virginia, an office complex large enough to accommodate all the members of Congress was hollowed out of a hill. It included a hospital, broadcast studios, a cafeteria, and a crematorium and was protected by 25-ton blast doors.[83] An underground Pentagon near Gettysburg existed at one time together with at least seventy-five presidential refuges at varying distances from the Capitol. All of these facilities were classified as Top Secret and only came into public view after they were abandoned. Today's comparable arrangements are thought to be even more elaborate.

One aspect of doomsday planning that was long concealed and continues to be shrouded in mystery today was the question of who was or is now authorized to order the launch of nuclear weapons. It is widely assumed that only the President has that prerogative, but, as previously noted, starting in 1957, pre-delegation authority was given to top commanders to launch a nuclear strike if the president or a recognized successor was not available [84] and, according to newspaper reports, the President's authority is currently shared with the Secretary of Defense.

The doomsday preparations of business corporations are likewise known mostly in retrospect. In the 1980s, numerous banks, oil companies, and other businesses established underground emergency headquarters from which to manage operations after a nuclear attack and found blast-proof locations for their records. Museums and libraries prepared to move their most valuable holdings to abandoned salt mines.

Throughout the Cold War, there was a running debate about the overall consequences for the United States of a nuclear war with the Soviet Union, which looked inevitable to many official planners and defense intellectuals, since they could not imagine a peaceful resolution of the ongoing conflict. Their forward vision was clouded by exaggerated estimates of the Soviet Union's economic and military strength but at the same time, they were reluctant to consider the possibility of a clear-cut American defeat. It was more or less illegal to do so. Reacting in 1958

to the title, not the unread content, of a RAND Corporation study called
Strategic Surrender, the Senate added an amendment to a defense appropriate bill forbidding the expenditure of federal funds to study any
hypothetical U.S. surrender.[85] Thus, for the most part, the defense intellectuals were unable to visualize any resolution of the Soviet-American
confrontation except war, or any Soviet-American war that did not involve a nuclear exchange, either initially or as an escalation by the losing side of a war begun with conventional weapons.

Ronald Reagan seems to have been the first political leader to imagine that the Cold War might end with the collapse of the Soviet Union.
He saw that the Soviet Union had lost its ideological appeal, was fading
economically and could no longer compete with the U.S. in military research and development. He foresaw the disintegration of the Soviet
empire and eventually, together with Mikhail Gorbachev, helped to
bring it about.

A half-century of misguided strategizing did not simply dissipate
when the Berlin Wall came down. The doomsday scenarios were
patched up for nuclear war with a resurgent Russia or with an emergent
China or with some combination of hostile states, and then retooled for
an endless war on terrorism and a clash of cultures with Islam. The
maintenance of a nuclear standoff between America and Russia has become an end in itself, unlinked to any important conflict of interest or
ideology. The Chinese show no disposition to take up the role of implacable enemy. They are too busy piling up enormous profits in their
commerce with the U.S. And while jihadists may conceivably obtain
and use nuclear weapons, they are not seriously expected to develop a
doomsday capacity. But Washington still plans for doomsday as if nothing had changed in the world since 1980.

Chapter Seven

Hostages and Tripwires

So far, we have considered only the favorable consequences of nuclear deterrence. It has permitted everyday life to continue in the five continents and on the seven seas as if the atom bomb had never been invented and the future of humanity was as securely grounded as its past. This book celebrates that great achievement.

But deterrence is a two-edged sword. It is encouraging to learn that terrorists seem to be subject to a measure of nuclear deterrence but less encouraging to realize that nuclear deterrence has a role in the terrorist playbook. The case of North Korea—a rogue state if ever there was one—makes this clear. North Korea in 2003 demonstrated the invulnerability of a nuclear-armed state by embarking on an ambitious program of uranium reprocessing, expelling the inspectors of the International Atomic Energy Agency and withdrawing from the non-proliferation regime, while trumpeting to the world its willingness to be bought off. Unlike the hypothetical nuclear threats from Iraq and Iran, the more plausible North Korean threat has, as of this writing, been convincing enough to deter any bellicose action by the U.S.

Al Qaeda and other more shadowy organizations with similar programs may lack the technical capacity to build a nuclear bomb or even the tactical capacity to steal one, but they certainly have the financial capacity to buy one. Currently, the most likely seller of military-grade warheads is the North Korean regime, which is short of hard currency and humanitarian sentiments, and has a record of building technically advanced missiles and offering them for sale to all comers. In 2006, North Korea was openly extracting plutonium from spent uranium fuel for the announced purpose of building an inventory of nuclear weapons and concurrently testing new models of long-range missiles. Blocking those nuclear preparations would be a challenging assignment under any circumstances but the local circumstances on the Korean peninsula are uniquely unfavorable. North Korea's conventional forces are out of all proportion to its weak economy and they are permanently poised to strike at the South Korean metropolis of Seoul only 50 miles from the border. An attack on North Korea by U.S. conventional or nuclear forces would risk the nuclear destruction of Seoul and its twelve million inhabitants.

This gigantic hostage situation is the joint creation of North Korea and the U.S.

An earlier North Korean attempt to extract a price for its nuclear potential was checked by the Agreed Framework of 1994, whereby North Korea agreed to halt its attempt to develop plutonium weapons in return for continuing supplies of fuel oil and two light-water power plants to be provided by the U.S. Both sides seem to have reneged on the agreement—the North Koreans by trying to produce fissile material by an alternative uranium route, the U.S. by delaying delivery of the promised power plants.

Meanwhile, the "sunshine policy" of cooperation adopted by South Korea began to show results. Land mines were removed along the border, South Koreans were allowed to visit relatives in the North, and a direct train connection was announced. When Kim Dae Jung, the principal architect of the sunshine policy, came to Washington to enlist support for the sunshine policy, he was publicly rebuffed. According to one observer:

> Bush disapproved of what he regarded as the appeasement of North Korea, and he was eager to establish a discontinuity with the Clinton administration. He also needed North Korea out in the cold in order to justify the first phase of the National Missile Defense program, the initial linchpin in the Bush strategy of asserting U.S. supremacy. Then came the "axis of evil" speech, and when North Korea surprised the Bush administration by admitting its uranium-enrichment program (strictly speaking not in violation of the Agreed Framework because that covered only plutonium) Bush cut off the supply of fuel oil. North Korea responded with various provocations.[86]

Thereafter, North Korea offered to abstain from both types of nuclear development in return for a non-aggression pact with the U.S. and the resumption of economic aid and asked for direct talks. The U.S. refused bilateral talks, announced that it would never yield to nuclear blackmail and called upon China, Russia, Japan and South Korea to exert pressure on North Korea. Six-power talks were organized and in In September 2005, the U.S. and North Korea announced an "agreement in principle" whereby North Korea agreed to give up its existing nuclear weapons and to return to the nuclear nonproliferation regime. The United States joined its four discussion partners in expressing respect for North Korea's "right to peaceful uses of nuclear energy" and promised energy assistance and economic cooperation. Within a day or two both sides were vigorously backpedaling . The North Koreans announced that they would surrender their nuclear weapons only after receiving the promised energy assistance. The U.S. disclaimed any intention of providing energy assistance before the weapons were given up. Although both sides had moved a good way from earlier positions. the talks seemed to have broken down until a new crisis developed in the summer of 2006 over North Korean missile tests. The North Koreans have actually detonated a nuclear device. They claim to have a few warheads and there seems to be some evidence supporting that claim.

Normal hostage situations begin with a ransom demand by the captors followed by a principled refusal by the authorities, who make the conventional announcement that ransom will not be paid under any circumstances. Then the negotiations begin. If the captors have no escape route, they become hostages themselves and must decide whether to murder their victims or surrender peaceably; that decision will turn on the terms offered for surrender. But if the victims are highly valued, a ransom (less than what was originally demanded) will eventually be paid and if the captors are surrounded, an escape route will be provided. Since the negotiations will be pervaded by mutual bad faith, it will sometimes happen that the ransom is paid and the hostages are murdered anyway, and it will sometimes happen that the safe escape route is a trap. But a situation that ends in the murder of the hostages is a failure for both sides, whether or not the captors survive. A flat refusal to negotiate in an ordinary hostage situation is self-defeating unless (a) the hostages are not valued by the authorities, or (b) there is a better than fair chance of rescuing the hostages by force.

A gigantic hostage situation exhibits much the same constraints. In Korea, the North Koreans are the captors; the people of Seoul are the hostages. The authorities are U.S. diplomats who have long since made and repeated the ritual announcement that no ransom will be paid. The refusal to negotiate was not absolute; the U.S. insisted on, and the North Koreans reluctantly agreed to, talks that included the four other Pacific powers.

In the end, ransom will probably be paid. Twelve million allied lives are more than we are prepared to sacrifice. The problem is how to guarantee the safe escape of the captors, who, once disarmed of nuclear weapons, will have a paranoid but understandable fear of American reprisal. Presumably, that guarantee can be provided by the four discussion partners if they are offered appropriate incentives. And if the ransom is well contrived, it will not be limited to supplies of fuel oil, but will aim at developing the North Korean economy towards eventual parity with the South.[87] In principle, that situation can be successfully resolved because the ransom demands are relatively modest.

What about other imaginable hostage situations? What if a nuclear device, authenticated in one way or another, is planted somewhere in San Francisco and the perpetrators demand a billion dollars to be wire transferred within 72 hours to an offshore account designated at the last moment and immediately dispersed from there to a hundred other offshore accounts? That ransom would probably be paid, followed by a heroic effort to track the money. What if a stolen Russian warhead, authenticated by serial number, is planted somewhere in Tel Aviv and the perpetrators demand the immediate release of all Palestinian prisoners held by Israel? That ransom would almost certainly be paid and followed by non-nuclear reprisals.The common element in every such situation is that nuclear deterrence would work in favor of the terrorists and eliminate the option of refusal, except in the unlikely case that the ransom exceeded the value of who or what was held hostage.

Tripwires create a special type of hostage situation produced by a gap in the nuclear rules. Rule Three (Any state may attack a non-nuclear state if the defending state has no nuclear guarantor) implies that a nuclear state may attack a non-nuclear state with its national forces, if the defending state has no nuclear guarantor. The Soviet invasion of Afghanistan, the Israeli invasions of Lebanon, the Kosovo operation, and the two American invasions of Iraq were all conformable with this rule. But the converse is less certain. Might a nuclear state, under certain circumstances, attack a non-nuclear state even though the defending state *did* have a nuclear guarantor?

The question was salient in the early days of the Cold War, when a Soviet invasion of western Europe seemed an imminent possibility. The United States stood nuclear guarantor to all of the threatened west European nations and to Germany in particular. But was the U.S. prepared to sacrifice Washington or New York in an effort to protect Bonn or Hamburg? Even though the object of nuclear deterrence is to prevent the use of nuclear weapons, its effectiveness depends upon a perceived willingness to use them after a given provocation. It was clear that the U.S. would not shrink from a nuclear reply to a nuclear attack on American territory or American troops, but whether the same response would be forthcoming in response to a nuclear attack on another country was less certain, no matter how many agreements to that effect were signed.

Britain and France met the problem by developing small but convincing nuclear arsenals of their own. Germany could not be allowed to do so. The problem was solved by positioning U.S. troops in the most likely path of a Soviet invasion, where they would serve as a tripwire. A Soviet attack on them would supposedly trigger an automatic nuclear response. The reassurance offered to the Europeans was less than perfect but good enough to be accepted.

The U.S. occupation forces stationed in postwar Germany eventually ceased to occupy that country or to monitor its political affairs but remained in place as a tripwire. A long-term commitment of American troops confirmed the nuclear guarantee extended to Japan. U.S. forces stayed in Korea to support an armed truce and came to be viewed as a tripwire protecting South Korea from an attack by North Korea.

Nuclear guarantees seem to work even without tripwires. An ambiguous U.S. guarantee has so far kept Taiwan safe from mainland China. Implied nuclear guarantees protect the Baltic nations against a much weakened Russia and all the nations of the western hemisphere against unidentified nuclear assailants.

So far then, nuclear states have not attacked non-nuclear states that have nuclear guarantors, even though the nuclear rules are a little ambiguous in such cases. Beijing may not believe that its forcible seizure of Taiwan would elicit a nuclear response from the U.S. but the marginal risk is too great to run. Here too, nuclear deterrence has been more effective than strict logic would anticipate.

Some defense intellectuals distinguished between central nuclear deterrence, exercised by a nuclear state on its own behalf and extended

nuclear deterrence, whereby a nuclear state guaranteed protection to
one or more non-nuclear states. The principal beneficiaries of extended
deterrence by the United States were South Korea, Japan and the west
European states belonging to NATO. There was much less emphasis on
extended deterrence by the Soviet Union, although the east European
states that adhered to the Warsaw Pact seemingly enjoyed the same
kind of nuclear protection as their NATO counterparts.

When the numbers game and the doctrine of Mutual Assured Destruction dominated nuclear strategy, the question of whether a guarantor state would actually risk its own destruction to protect a foreign
client became one of great concern to defense intellectuals who doubted
that a response to a nuclear attack on a third party would be automatic
if it really involved the mutual destruction of both the attacker and the
guarantor.[88] The theoretical issue was complicated by the fact that the
case of extended deterrence most often discussed was the nuclear guarantee of western European states by the U.S., which was atypical because western Europe included nuclear-armed third parties: Britain,
which was a junior partner in the original development of the atom
bomb and France, which became a nuclear-weapons state soon after.
Their relatively small but deadly thermonuclear arsenals provided another layer of extended deterrence to their NATO partners as well as
protection for themselves over and above the U.S. nuclear guarantee.

There is also some question as to whether the critics of extended deterrence were correct in assuming that the response to a nuclear attack on
a client state or the crossing of a tripwire would not be automatic. Although some details are classified, it appears that during the Cold War,
an American second strike would have been forthcoming even if the U.S.
government had been decapitated by a Soviet first strike. For many years
an airplane code-named Looking Glass flew random patterns above the
Midwest carrying an Air Force general with the necessary communications equipment to launch a nuclear second strike if higher national authorities were put out of action. Other arrangements were in place to assure that a Soviet nuclear attack on any of the third-party states under
U.S. protection would evoke a virtually automatic response. Even today,
as previously noted, the American response to a hostile nuclear attack,
whether directed at the homeland or at a NATO ally or at a tripwire,
would probably be immediate and overwhelming.

Chapter Eight

Nuclear Restraints

The Cuban missile crisis of 1962 was the turning point of the Cold War. After nearly stumbling into a nuclear conflict, the United States and the Soviet Union were much more disposed to negotiate nuclear issues. Since then, nuclear arms control has proceeded along two separate but roughly parallel tracks—bilateral treaties between the United States and the Soviet Union (or Russia) and multilateral treaties open to all nations.

On the bilateral track, the two superpowers regulated their arms race by treaty to their mutual advantage until the breakup of the Soviet Union, whereupon the Russian Federation took over and the bargaining continued on its own momentum into a fantasyland where the sole superpower and the ex-superpower continue to threaten each other with total devastation for no apparent reason. Both sides are committed to further reductions in their nuclear arsenals but that commitment is nullified by a huge loophole in the most recent agreement.

On the multilateral track, most of the world's independent nations have ratified three major agreements intended to discourage nuclear proliferation: the Limited Test Ban Treaty of 1963, the Nuclear Non-Proliferation Treaty of 1970, and the Comprehensive Test Ban Treaty of 1996, which has not yet gone into effect.

The first of a series of bilateral agreements[89] between the United States and the Soviet Union was the Anti Ballistic Missile Treaty of 1972, which limited each side to two local anti-ballistic missile systems (later reduced to one) and prohibited any upgrading of their components. The stated purpose was to "decrease the pressures of technological change and its unsettling impact on the strategic balance,"[90] i.e. to preserve the second-strike vulnerability of both sides. The preamble to the treaty mentioned among other premises, "that nuclear war would have devastating consequences for all mankind" and " that the limitation of anti-ballistic missile systems . . . would contribute to further negotiations on limiting strategic arms."[91] It even mentioned the parties' intentions to proceed eventually to general and complete disarmament. The United States withdrew from the agreement in 2002 to clear the way for the National Missile Defense Initiative, the current successor to Star Wars.

The Strategic Arms Limitation Treaty (SALT I), which went into effect in the same year, froze the number of ballistic missile launchers (but not the number of warheads) at existing levels and provided that new submarine launchers could be added only after the same number of older launchers were taken out of service. The SALT II agreement of 1979 emerged from a seven-year round of talks between the parties. It too limited the number of long-range missile launchers but not the number of warheads, for a period of five years, thus stimulating the development of missiles carrying multiple nuclear warheads (MIRVs). The treaty also restricted intermediate range cruise missiles and bombers. Displeasure with the Soviet invasion of Afghanistan blocked U.S. ratification of this treaty but its terms were honored anyway.

Up to that point, the experiment of nuclear arms control paralleled the experience of naval disarmament that had begun with the Washington Naval Conference in 1922 and continued into the 1930s. In that earlier series of conferences and negotiations, the parties did not agree to end their arms race but did submit it to regulation. After the Washington Conference fixed the relative strength of the naval powers in battleships, their efforts shifted to the unrestricted construction of cruisers, submarines and destroyers. After the SALT agreements fixed the strength of the parties in missile launchers, attention shifted to increasing the number and accuracy of the warheads delivered by each launcher.

The first arms control agreement between the United States and the Soviet Union that involved an actual reduction in offensive arms was the Intermediate Range Nuclear Forces Treaty signed by Reagan and Gorbachev in 1987, which banned an entire class of nuclear weapons that both sides had deployed in the European theater. It eliminated all ground-based ballistic and cruise missiles with ranges up to 500 kilometers together with their supporting facilities. Even more significantly, this treaty allowed each side to inspect the other's installations and monitor compliance with the treaty.

The Strategic Arms Reduction Treaty (START II) signed in December 1991 committed the United States and the Russian Federation to reduce their deployed strategic nuclear warheads to 6000 apiece over seven years. It eventually involved the three successor states—Belarus, Ukraine, and Kazakhstan—that had inherited bits and pieces of the Soviet nuclear arsenal. They agreed to give these up and to join the non-proliferation regime as non-weapons states. By December 2001, the three successor states were nuclear-free and the two principal powers were close to their agreed levels of deployed strategic warheads, although that achievement was less important than it seemed, given the thin line between deployed and stored warheads.

The treaty included provisions for intrusive verification, including data exchange, twelve types of on-site inspection and continuous monitoring. American inspectors became familiar figures at Russian assembly sites and Russian inspectors were entitled to similar access in the U.S.

Although bipolar negotiations looking to a START III and even a START IV agreement went forward in the 1990s, no important new agreements were reached until the Bush-Putin summit of 2001 and the resulting Treaty of Moscow in May 2002. Though presented as an arms reduction treaty, this was a backward step in the long, slow process of nuclear disarmament. The parties agreed to reduce their deployed strategic warheads to the range of 1700 to 2200 on each side by the end of 2012, but the U.S. stipulated against strong Russian objections, that the weapons taken out of service would be placed in reserve, not destroyed. Russia had suggested that both governments destroy not just launchers, as previously, but warheads also. The U.S. was adamantly opposed.[92] Both sides are free to define the composition and structure of their offensive forces within the imposed ceilings.

It should be noted that the various agreements aimed at reducing the two major nuclear arsenals apply only to strategic weapons and systems,[93] those involving the long-range delivery of thermonuclear weapons by bombers, land-based ballistic missiles, submarine-based ballistic missiles and cruise missiles. Both the U.S. and Russia still have thousands of smaller nuclear weapons that are not covered by agreements of any kind.

The first and most effective multilateral agreement in the nuclear area was the Limited Test Ban Treaty of 1963. In that historic document, the United States, the Soviet Union and the United Kingdom agreed to abandon nuclear testing above ground, under water and in outer space and invited all other nations to join. Underground testing was permitted provided that no radioactive debris escaped the tester's territory. The treaty went into effect as soon as it was accepted by its three sponsors, to run indefinitely. More than a thousand nuclear tests had by then been conducted in the atmosphere and there was widespread concern about radioactive fallout. The ban was also understood to be an effective way to discourage nuclear proliferation. And so it proved to be. As of 2005, 113 states had signed the treaty and all but 17 had ratified it. There seem not to have been any violations. (France, the principal practitioner of tests in the atmosphere after 1963, never joined.) Moreover, this treaty set the pattern for other multilateral treaties to restrict weapons of mass destruction in one way or another, including agreements barring nuclear weapons from outer space, from the sea bed, and from Africa, Latin America and the South Pacific.

A later and less successful attempt to discourage the testing of nuclear weapons was the Comprehensive Test Ban Treaty, which was negotiated by the United States, the United Kingdom and the Russian Federation in 1996, with an invitation for all other nations to join. It would ban all nuclear tests above, below or on the world's surface. As of 2006, it had been signed by 176 states and ratified by 125, but was not in force and its prospects were poor. Unlike the Limited Test Ban Treaty, which went into effect without delay, its comprehensive successor will not be operative until it has been ratified by all of the 44 nations having nuclear installations of any kind. Among the 11 nations with nuclear installations that have not ratified the treaty and can block it indefinitely are the United States, China, Iran, and Israel.

The United States, together with 186 other nations, participates in the nonproliferation regime administered by the International Atomic Energy Agency (IAEA), headquartered in Vienna. Established by the United Nations in 1957 to promote the peaceful use of nuclear energy, it took on the more critical function of preventing nuclear proliferation under the Nuclear Nonproliferation Treaty of 1968.[94] That treaty was short and sweet, barely three pages long. It proposed a bargain between the so-called weapons-states, (United States, Soviet Union, Britain,

France, and China) which had acquired nuclear weapons before 1967 and all other nations. Each weapons-state agreed not to transfer nuclear weapons to any non-weapons-state or sub-national group and not to assist any non-weapons-state to acquire such weapons. By ratifying the treaty, a non-weapons-state agreed not to acquire nuclear weapons or components and not to help others to do so. All parties were to have full access to nuclear technology for peaceful purposes and the treaty contains a clause to that effect that figures largely in current negotiations with North Korea and Iran:

> Nothing in this Treaty shall be interpreted as affecting the inalienable right of all the parties to the Treaty to develop research, production and use of nuclear energy for peaceful purposes without discrimination . . .[95]

The quid pro quo that the weapons-states offered to the non-weapons-states in return for their nuclear abstinence was the promise of nuclear disarmament:

> Each of the Parties to this Treaty undertakes to pursue negotiations in good faith on effective measures relating to cessation of the nuclear arms race at an early date and to nuclear disarmament, and on a Treaty on general and complete disarmament under strict and effective international control.[96]

The promise of general and complete disarmament was probably not intended to be taken literally. What moved most national governments to sign on to the treaty and agree to do without nuclear weapons seemed to be deterrence in another form. Their fear of nuclear weapons in the hands of their neighbors was greater than their interest in acquiring their own.

The nonproliferation regime has not been ineffective. The IAEA membership includes a number of states—like Japan, Germany and Brazil—that were and are capable of developing nuclear weapons on their own but have elected to abstain. South Africa actually manufactured half a dozen nuclear bombs and then destroyed them and reverted to non-weapons status. Ukraine, Kazakhstan and Belarus chose to give up the nuclear weapons they inherited in the breakup of the Soviet Union. More recently, Libya abandoned a promising nuclear program under American pressure.[97] The three known proliferators, Israel, India, and Pakistan, and the two would-be proliferators, North Korea and Iran, all plead special circumstances.

As to proliferation, both India and Pakistan conducted successful nuclear tests in the spring of 1998, while Israel has long been recognized as an unofficial weapons-state. More recently, Iraq, North Korea and Iran, the three axis-of-evil states named by President Bush, have pursued nuclear weapons development. The Iraqi program was abandoned at some time after the first Gulf War but the North Korean and Iranian programs are still active.

The three current proliferators and the two would-be proliferators are anomalous in relation to the non-proliferation regime, since they are neither recognized weapons-states nor non-weapons-states. The anomaly was compounded by the India-U.S. Joint Statement of July 2005 in which the U.S. undertook to adjust its laws, policies and international commitments in order to permit full civil nuclear energy cooperation and trade with India, a non-member of the IAEA. To some observers, this was a significant shift away from the long-standing American policy of support for nonproliferation,[98] although federal spokesmen on other wavelengths, such as the Undersecretary of State for Arms Control and International Security and the White House Press Secretary were simultaneously proclaiming the administration's fervent attachment to the principle of nonproliferation.

The presence of three weapons-states and two would-be weapons-states outside of the nonproliferation regime might seem to indicate that nonproliferation was going out of style, and a few ingenious commentators have argued that wider proliferation might somehow make for a safer world. A closer look at the five cases suggests (1) that under the nonproliferation regime, proliferation is a very slow and difficult process requiring foreign assistance; (2) that the motives for proliferation in these five cases were apparently defensive; (3) that the nuclear arsenals of the proliferators are not in any way comparable to those of the recognized weapons-states; but (4) that it does not take much of a nuclear arsenal to achieve effective deterrence.

The advent of weapons-states outside the jurisdiction of the IAEA poses a challenge to the nonproliferation regime by showing that it can be defied with relative impunity by any state actually possessing a few nuclear weapons. On the other hand, it is doubtful that the five recognized weapons-states have kept their part of the original bargain, whereby they offered nuclear disarmament in return for the continuation of their nuclear monopoly. While general and complete disarmament was perhaps chimerical, the non-weapons-states might well have expected a greater reduction of the weapons-states' nuclear arsenals than has so far occurred.

The Israeli nuclear weapons program dates back to 1949, when scientists in the Israeli Defense Force explored the Negev desert for sources of uranium. Serious work on nuclear technology got underway in the early 1950s with important assistance from France, which provided a powerful nuclear reactor for an atomic center at Dimona. The U.S. identified Dimona as a nuclear site in 1960 but took no action. It was later reported that Israel had two bombs available during the Six Day War of 1967 and 13 bombs in readiness during the Yom Kippur War of 1973. Van Creveld speculates that the mere suspicion that Israel might have atomic bombs deterred Syria and Egypt from attacking Israel's home territory in 1973.[99] In any case, it is clear that ever since, deterrence against hostile national forces has worked very well for Israel, vastly outnumbered by unfriendly neighbors. Current estimates credit Israel with between 100 and 200 warheads,[100] deliverable by plane or missile.

India's nuclear history goes back nearly as far. In the mid 1950s, India acquired dual-use technologies under the "Atoms for Peace" program, which offered support for peaceful applications of nuclear energy in return for assurances that they would not be turned to military use. India's heavy water reactor was acquired from Canada and its heavy water from the U.S. under that program. Diversion to military use began in 1964 with the commissioning of a facility to separate plutonium. Plutonium fueled India's "peaceful nuclear explosion" in 1974.

There followed a long pause until March 1998 when India tested five nuclear devices underground, in response to a Pakistani missile test. One device was claimed to be thermonuclear but the claim was not confirmed by seismic evidence. Three of the tests yielded fractions of a kiloton. India is currently estimated to have about 60 nuclear warheads, all of them intended for Pakistan, but none actually targeted. The warheads are said to be stored separately from their delivery vehicles.[101]

Pakistan's nuclear weapons program goes back to 1972 but acquired new momentum after India's "peaceful nuclear explosion" of 1974. The notorious Dr. Khan arrived in Pakistan in 1975, bringing with him gas centrifuge technology developed in the Netherlands and enrichment technology stolen elsewhere in Europe. Pakistan was producing weapons-grade uranium as early as 1985 but refrained from testing until India's five tests in May 1998. Within two weeks, Pakistan replied with six tests of its own. The most powerful of these devices had an estimated yield of 9-12 kilotons; other yields were much lower. Meanwhile, Dr. Khan continued to sell nuclear technology and equipment on the international black market until his activities came to light in 2004. Pakistan's is currently estimated to have between 24 and 48 warheads, and like India, is believed to store its warheads and delivery vehicles separately.[102]

The two would-be proliferators, North Korea and Iran, have barely arrived at the nuclear threshold. Both programs are shrouded in secrecy and both go a long way back.

North Korea's nuclear efforts date to the 1980s but were supposed to be halted by the Agreed Framework negotiated with the U.S. in 1994. Although a plutonium program was duly suspended, a concealed uranium program continued. In 2002, North Korea responded to its designation as part of the axis-of-evil by withdrawing from the Nuclear Nonproliferation Treaty, expelling the IAEA inspectors and resuming the suspended plutonium program. As noted in the previous chapter, a six-nation consortium is currently attempting to negotiate the permanent abandonment of all of North Korea's nuclear weapons activities. The North Koreans are believed to have a few warheads.

Iran, also a designated axis-of-evil state, has been engaged for some years in an effort to obtain fissile materials by the gas centrifuge method, ostensibly for electricity production. IEAE inspectors have found a number of secret installations and suspect that others remain undiscovered. In 2003, the British, French and German foreign ministers negotiated an agreement with Iran for the suspension of all uranium-enrichment activities, but Iran resumed those activities in 2005, alleging that the benefits promised by the European Union had not been delivered. The U.S. joined the negotiations in 2005 and was actively negotiating with Iran in 2006, while simultaneously threatening sanctions and/or military action. There is still no direct evidence that Iran is attempting to develop nuclear weapons or any accurate estimate of how long that might take.[103]

It is now more than forty years since the United States and the Soviet Union began to negotiate limits on their frenetic preparations for mutual assured destruction. In the course of that frenzy, the United States manufactured more than 70,000 nuclear bombs and warheads and built 4,680 heavy bombers and 67,500 missiles to carry the bombs and warheads[104] to enemy territory. The Soviet Union, after a late start, more than matched these extraordinary numbers. After a generation's worth of arms control agreements, after the metamorphosis of the menacing Soviet Union into the unmenacing Russian Federation, and after the Cold War had been replaced by a "strategic partnership," each side still aimed thousand of strategic weapons at the other.[105] If the terms of the Treaty of Moscow are actually carried out by the year 2012, each side will have retained about 2000 strategic warheads and have the means to destroy all of the other's cities and most of the other's population several times over, together with an unchallengeable second-strike capability.

The failure of the Cold War to turn into a shooting war demonstrated the surprising effectiveness of nuclear deterrence. The current Cooled War is more mysterious. No strategic theory explains it. No national interest requires it. But nobody in authority questions it. Official Washington is far more concerned about the nuclear threat from North Korea.

The Russian nuclear arsenal seems to be viewed as a decaying relic of Soviet power. The facts available in this era of transparency[106] tell a different story. Russia, it seems, is busy modernizing its intercontinental ballistic missiles, reducing the number of types from five to two, including one new type, and discarding older liquid-fueled missiles. It currently deploys 12 nuclear submarines armed with strategic missiles and two new submarines are under construction. It has 78 nuclear bombers in service and is building new ones. An advanced cruise missile is ready for deployment. Russian forces conducted 15 missile tests in 2004. Counting non-strategic weapons, Russia still has about 16,000 intact nuclear warheads, down from about 35,000 at the end of the Cold War. These numbers may not be accurate—counts of nuclear weapons are never entirely consistent or trustworthy—but the order of magnitude is presumably correct.

The U.S. officially acknowledged 7,000 active strategic warheads in 2005, with more in reserve,[107] down from 32,193 in 1966. [108] The triad of bombers, land-based missiles and submarine-based missiles is still maintained in full, and in each of these categories, the U.S. arsenal is

presumed superior to the Russian arsenal in quality, although not in explosive yield. The strategic nuclear weapons deployed by the U.S. and
Russia are in a range far above the Hiroshima and Nagasaki bombs and
the 10- or 20-kiloton bombs of the proliferators. They are thermonuclear weapons yielding from 100 kilotons up into the multi-megaton
range.

Thus, long years after peace was made between the United States and
the Soviet Union, the nuclear sword of Damocles still hangs over us—
the possibility of an accidental or intentional first strike in either direction and the likelihood of a second-strike response. That is more of a
strain than nuclear deterrence should be forced to bear, considering how
little is achieved and how much is risked by the Cooled War.

The three other nuclear arsenals[109] that claim legitimacy under the
nonproliferation regime deserve notice. China has apparently been
moving away from restraint, by increasing the size, accuracy, range and
survivability of its nuclear weapons, and by imitating the U.S. and Soviet triads of missiles launched from planes, silos and submarines, although their one nuclear submarine may not be operational and their
ballistic missiles may not carry multiple warheads. But all of their
strategic weapons are in the thermonuclear range and no one doubts
their ability to develop the entire triad. As of 2003, they were thought
to have a total of about 250 strategic weapons of which a few might be
able to reach the United States. A more recent estimate suggests that the
total may be closer to 100 and that the recent improvements may be exaggerated.[110] More than any other weapons-state, the People's Republic
insists on its devotion to arms control, disarmament and nonproliferation.[111] France meanwhile has abandoned the triad in favor of strategic
weapons launched from submarines and aircraft, with a strong prefer-
ence for submarines. Its submarine-launched thermonuclear weapons
have a maximum range of 4000 miles and are equipped for precision
guidance. The United Kingdom has gone the furthest in exploiting the
invulnerability of missiles launched from nuclear-powered submarines.
With approximately 200 thermonuclear warheads, each yielding 100
kilotons and having a range of 5,000 miles, and all based on submarines, Britain now has a nuclear deterrent essentially equal to any
other, although its weapons are not kept on high alert. Submarines being highly mobile, the 5,000-mile range of the British Tridents brings
every country and city in the world within their destructive reach. It is

hard to understand why a more powerful deterrent would ever be needed by any national state.

If nuclear deterrence is so effective, a critic of the nonproliferation regime might ask, why would it not be advantageous for every national government that could afford the expense to acquire a few nuclear weapons and become immune to attack by the armed forces of any other nation? The question sounds foolish but deserves an answer.

The most obvious objection to wider proliferation is that it would greatly increase the risk of nuclear terrorism, which given the multitude of actors and motives, cannot be as reliably deterred as international wars. The possibility that Saddam Hussein might sell nuclear warheads to Islamic terrorists if he ever acquired them himself was frequently mentioned as a justification for the U.S. invasion of Iraq, despite long-standing issues between the secular Baathists and the anti-secular jihadists. The more realistic possibility that North Korea might do the same has never been absent from the negotiations about that country's nuclear program, since North Korea has sold missiles to foreigners without regard for geopolitical consequences. Iran's nuclear ambitions arouse the same concerns more acutely, since the Iranian regime has close ties to the jihad movement.

Another objection to wide proliferation stems from an ambiguity in the unwritten rules that do not seem to prohibit a nuclear attack by a nuclear-armed state against a non-nuclear state that has no nuclear guarantor. So far, this contingency has been blocked by the enormous power of the five recognized weapons-states in relation to any non-nuclear state by which they might be threatened and by the special circumstances that keep the current proliferators on the defensive.

To suppose that the same restraints would apply to every future proliferator, if proliferation became general, would be wildly optimistic.

Chapter Nine

Regulating War

The world of 1900 was governed directly or indirectly by Europeans and people of European descent. The only countries that had escaped that condition were Japan, Ethiopia and Yemen. Japan[112] had done it by adopting European military technology; the others were protected by isolation, harsh terrain and tribal ferocity.

The Eurocentric world of 1900 counted six great powers. Britain, France, Austria-Hungary and Russia had survived the Napoleonic wars. Germany and Italy had been formed by the consolidation of smaller sovereignties during the nineteenth century. The United States and Japan were about to be promoted to great power status by the settlement of the Russo-Japanese war in 1905—Japan as the victor and the U.S. as the mediator of that important conflict. A half-dozen minor powers—Belgium, the Netherlands, Spain, Portugal, Sweden, Denmark, Serbia, Siam, Persia, Brazil—made up the supporting cast. Two ancient, ramshackle empires—the Ottoman and the Chinese—figured largely in the calculations of the European powers because of their military vulnerability.

The great powers were so called because each of them had the capacity for independent military action. Germany, France, Russia, Austria-Hungary and Italy had large conscript armies. Britain, Germany, France, Italy, the United States and Japan had powerful navies. Each of the minor powers had a sizeable army and several of them sported colonial empires.

The long-term goal of each great power was to prevent any other great power from dominating the international system. The emperor

Charles V in the sixteenth century, Louis XIV in the seventeenth century, Napoleon in the early nineteenth century, had come close to achieving domination but each of their attempts had provoked the formation of a hostile coalition that eventually prevailed. As a prominent British historian wrote during World War I.

> Four times in four centuries, have the Nation States of Europe been compelled to combine against the threatened domination of one of their number . . . Against the fourth attempt to enthrall Europe—and not Europe only—we are still in arms.[113]

In the early years of the twentieth century, the contest for domination had seemed to be in remission. The few European wars fought between 1815 and 1914 were short and relatively cheap. The only wars that produced heaped corpses and burnt out cities during that long interval - the American Civil War, the Lopez War in Paraguay, the Taiping Rebellion in China—were outside the arena of great power competition. It seemed likely that war would soon disappear from the annals of the advanced nations along with other barbaric practices inherited from the past: slavery and the slave trade, human sacrifice, judicial torture, female infanticide, the persecution of witches, blood feuds, burning at the stake, piracy, serfdom, child labor, imprisonment for debt, the castration of boy sopranos in Rome, and the plundering of shipwrecks on the New England coast.

In 1907, representatives of all the governments in the world had any significant military assets met at the Hague to finalize a general revision of the rules of war. By then, every one of the powers, even despotic states like Russia and backward states like Spain, displayed such liberal trends as the enlargement of the franchise, the improvement of workplace conditions, the softening of punishments for crime, the suppression of private violence, and the expansion of social services.

The cruelties of war had been much softened also. The press gang, flogging and keel-hauling were no longer part of naval practice. The accepted rules of land warfare now prohibited the sack and pillage of captured towns, the killing of enemy wounded, the enslavement of prisoners, the taking of hostages, the massacre of noncombatants and the seizure of private property without compensation. Although European wars had previously been fought under customary rules, those rules had been more concerned with the privileges of officers than with

the protection of noncombatants, neutrals and common soldiers. Captured officers could give their paroles and move about freely until ex-
changed while their men were confined in stinking dungeons or casu-
ally slaughtered. Defeated commanders were allowed to keep their
personal effects while captured cities were mercilessly plundered.

But the latter half of the nineteenth century and the opening years of
the twentieth witnessed a remarkable international effort to reform the
conduct of war by means of multilateral treaties. The revised standards
created by these treaties were remarkably humane compared to earlier
practices, The Declaration of Paris in 1856 prohibited privateering and
defined the rights of neutrals. The Red Cross Convention of 1864 guaranteed immunity from hostile action to medical personnel, ambulances,
dressing stations, hospitals, hospital ships and wounded prisoners. The
Declaration of St. Petersburg in 1868 outlawed explosive bullets. The
unratified Declaration of Brussels in 1874 enlarged the rights of prisoners of war. [114]

The grand finale of the international effort to mitigate the rigors of
war came in two parts: the Hague Conferences of 1899 and 1907, originally convened by—of all people - the Russian Czar. The numerous
treaties drafted at the 1899 conference were signed by every one of the
European powers, as well as the United States, Japan, China, Persia and
Siam. One of the 1899 treaties limited the use of military force for the
collection of debts and prohibited the opening of hostilities without a
formal declaration of war. Another banned poison gas. Another stipulated that prisoners of war must be as well fed, clothed and housed as
their captors. Other Hague treaties covered spies, ruses, truces, capitu-
lations and restrictions on the conduct of occupation forces. An especially ambitious treaty provided for the peaceful settlement of international disputes and established a permanent Court of Arbitration for that
purpose.

When the conference was reconvened at the Hague in 1907, ten more
treaties were signed by representatives of all the governments that then
had any significant military capacity. They covered the rights and duties
of neutral states and their citizens, the status of enemy merchant ships
at the outbreak of hostilities, the laying of submarine mines, limits on
naval bombardment, the adaptation of the Red Cross protection to naval
forces, further restrictions on the right of capture in naval operations, an
international prize court and—most notably—an agreement to prohibit

"the discharge of projectiles and explosives from balloons or by other new methods of a similar nature" that was to remain in effect until the Third Hague Peace Conference (which was never held.)

The Hague delegates took for granted that international war would soon be consigned to the dustbin of history. In the meantime, they meant to civilize it. The project was not absurd in the light of what was then known. In the ninety-odd years since the battle of Waterloo, the nation-states of Europe had indeed adopted higher standards of conduct in their mutual relations. There were few ideological disagreements among them at the time and no outside power presented a military threat. The perennial European conflict between conservatives and revolutionaries and the newer conflict between capital and labor were only marginally connected to issues of peace and war.[115]

Might the Hague expectations have been realized if the decision-makers of 1914-1918 had made different decisions? The question is debatable.

The negative argument is easier to make. The dynamics of the great power game had not changed. One great power—Germany in this case—saw an opportunity to achieve domination; the other great powers would reflexively resist. The great powers were firmly committed to a naval arms race while their recently formed general staffs routinely scripted wars with every possible adversary and their meticulous plans, tied to railroad time tables and factory production schedules, were inflexible. Indeed, the German experience of 1914 showed that even the Kaiser himself could not interrupt a mobilization in progress.

All through the nineteenth century, the rise of chauvinistic nationalism had kept pace with the spread of liberal social policies, especially in the subject territories of the Austro-Hungarian and Ottoman empires, but also elsewhere in Europe. Each emerging nationality—Bulgarian, Rumanian, Finnish, Armenian, Serbian, Albanian, Polish, Greek, Lithuanian, Catalan, Basque—sought independence by armed insurrection, no other route being known. Each great power encouraged a nationalist movement of its own, partly in defense against separatist movements, partly to sustain the morale of its armed forces.

Together, the negative argument runs, these two conditions made it inevitable that the effort to regulate war would fail. That view gains color from the astonishing jubilation that accompanied the outbreak of World War I in August 1914. The patriotic fervor of both sides was not confined to the cheering masses. Among the surprising enthusiasts for the war were Mahatma Gandhi, Igor Stravinsky, Henry James, Sigmund Freud and Max Weber.[116]

The positive argument is more nuanced and rests on the assumption that the short, relatively painless war anticipated by both sides in August 1914 could easily have occurred and would not have permanently altered the balance of power, since British naval superiority would have blocked the German drive to dominance, whether France had been defeated in a short, painless war or the Germans had withdrawn from France after the first Battle of the Marne in the autumn of 1914. Thereafter, the march towards international comity might well have resumed.

As the war churned on without a resolution, it became increasingly irrational for all of the participants. The only reason for continuing was that the sunk costs at each stage were so great that to walk away without victory would have been politically fatal for the leaders.No one in authority in 1914 seems to have anticipated how high those costs would eventually mount, although a closer look at the American Civil War might have given them clues. That had been the first war in which railroads enabled mass armies to keep the field year round; the electric telegraph enhanced command and control; automatic weapons mowed down infantry formations like ripe corn; observers in tethered balloons directed artillery strikes from high above the battlefield and the sunk costs rose so high that the fighting continued long after the issue was decided. In the fifty years after Appomattox, the industrialization of war had advanced much further. Motor vehicles supplemented the railroads. Communication by field telephone and radio replaced the crude telegraphy of the 1860s. Machine guns threw much greater showers of lead than the early Gatling guns. Explosive shells replaced cannon balls and bombardment from the air became routine. Then, less than a decade after the solemn adoption of the Hague program to regulate war, the killing began in earnest.

When Pitirim Sorokin examined the military experience of France, England, Austria-Hungary and Russia through several centuries, he discovered that the casualty rates (killed, wounded and missing) in their armies increased from about six percent in the wars of the sixteenth century to about 40 percent in World War I.[117]

Sorokin's figures covered only four of the European powers. Other authors[118] estimated that the nations involved in World War I mobilized about 65 million men, of whom about eight million were killed by hostile action and another five million died in service. In grim contrast to previous wars, nearly as many noncombatants as soldiers were killed by hostile action from 1914 to 1918. Untold numbers of men, women and children were wounded or made homeless. Millions lived on with crippling disabilities.

World War II began as another effort to prevent the domination of the international system by Germany. It raised the stakes much further. The total mobilization for that war was over 100 million with about 15 million military dead and about 30 million civilians killed by hostile action. To complete the toll of the blood-soaked twentieth century, we must add the dead of the Paraguay-Bolivia War of 1928-35, the Sino-Japanese War that began in 1931, the Spanish Civil War of 1936-39, the three India-Pakistan wars over Kashmir, the Korean War of 1950-53, the two Vietnam Wars, the Iran-Iraq War of 1980-87 and the 1979-1989 Soviet occupation of Afghanistan, together with the casualties of some 52 civil wars that raged in the latter half of the twentieth century.

Zbigniew Brezezinski calculated that the wars of the twentieth century extinguished about 87 million lives, with the numbers of wounded, maimed or otherwise afflicted "beyond estimate." Along with the increased lethality of war came the astounding lethality of totalitarian politics. To Hitler's holocaust of the European Jews and his murder of Gypsies and Poles, Brezezinski would add the mass executions and induced famines of the Soviet era, the casualties of forcible collectivization and the Cultural Revolution in China and the millions of victims claimed by lesser genocidal regimes from Armenia to Cambodia. He concludes that the total of those killed deliberately—not in combat but in cold blood—for various ideological and religious reasons during the twentieth century came to upwards of 80 million more. His figures, published in 1993, do not include the more recent massacres in Rwanda, Bosnia, Somalia, Congo, Liberia, Sudan, Darfur and other killing fields.[119]

The rejection of the Hague scenario could hardly have been more complete. The Hague rules of war were not entirely disregarded in World War I, since the violation of Belgian neutrality, the shelling of cathedrals, the use of poison gas and unrestricted submarine warfare were recognized as infractions by the perpetrators, who pleaded military necessity. But World War II witnessed the wholesale abandonment of restraint—passenger ships sunk without warning, the enslavement of enemy civilians, the resumption of mass rape and pillage, the massacre of war prisoners, the deliberate demolition of cultural monuments.

The most consequential breach of the rules was the routine use of military force against noncombatants. There was an insidious progression from the carpet bombing of Rotterdam and Coventry by the Germans in 1940, which aroused universal outrage, to the Allied firebombing of Hamburg in 1943 and the American firebombing of Tokyo in 1945, which aroused no outrage to speak of. The slaughter of women and children had become ordinary acts of war without even the lame excuse of military necessity.[120]

Because it occurred gradually and was shielded by the normal xenophobia of nations at war, the moral desensitization that permitted God-fearing Americans and Englishmen to rain death and destruction on German residential districts far from any military target went unnoticed. The sinking of Japanese merchant ships in the Pacific by U.S. submarines without any care for the survival of their crews was construed as a reasonable response to the similar acts of German U-boats in the Atlantic. The flattening of German cities was regarded as just revenge for the sufferings inflicted on Londoners by the Luftwaffe. The firebombing of Tokyo was seen as payback for Pearl Harbor. And after the killing of hundreds of thousands of Japanese civilians in the air raids of early 1945, the step to nuclear incineration was easy

The century-long effort to restrain the fury of war by international agreement had been a catastrophic failure. But new constraints on international war, grounded on wholesome fear rather than good intentions, were about to appear.

From the beginning, the industrialization of war had achieved a progressive reduction in the economic cost of ending a human life and a parallel reduction in the cost of destroying artifacts. The invention of nuclear weapons further decreased those costs by many orders of magnitude and raised the prospect of holocausts unmatched in history. But the practical consequences were just the reverse. Wars between nuclear-armed nations did not happen—although nobody seemed to notice.

As World War II wound down, it became apparent that only two great powers were left. France and Britain, nominally victorious, retained only nominal military assets. Germany and Italy had none at all. The Soviet army loomed over Europe while America owned the Bomb and the planes to deliver it anywhere. Meanwhile, the dynamic of the great power game reasserted itself. With only two players left, the goal of each was to prevent the other from achieving domination. In the beginning, the conflict was asymmetrical. The vast Soviet army, which was still in the process of seizing control of eastern Europe, could have swept across western Europe at pleasure, with or without the help of the large communist parties that flourished in Italy and France. But the U.S. Air Force had the means to demolish Moscow and Leningrad in response. Unsure of the adversary's intentions, each side began to work its way towards symmetry. With the help of subversive western scientists, the Soviets developed an atom bomb of their own by 1949, while the United States reversed demobilization and expanded its land and naval forces. Both sides recruited allies—in NATO and the Warsaw Pact—for the hypothetical war that could not be fought because of the foreseeable consequences. For more than forty years, two great armies faced each other on the North German plain, each alert for action and bristling with conventional and nuclear weapons, but never a shot was fired in anger. Each side ceaselessly designed and redesigned its battle plans without being able to find a formula for victory over a nuclear-armed adversary. In the long history of warfare, nothing like this had ever happened before.

The consensus of the military planners was that if the Cold War became hot, both sides would use nuclear weapons and each side would sustain casualties in the tens or hundreds of millions. Neither side could win but one side might "prevail." Attention thus shifted to the dubious goal of prevailing by means of quantitative superiority. Both sides developed thermonuclear weapons with explosive yields vastly greater than the Hiroshima bomb. Both sides progressed from short-range to intercontinental missiles and from single warheads to clusters of separately targeted warheads carried on a single missile. Both sides devised ways of launching missiles from invulnerable submarines. Both sides developed nuclear weapons small enough to be carried in a backpack but powerful enough to devastate a battlefield. Both sides yielded to political pressures from their armed forces to keep obsolete weapons and delivery vehicles in service. The results were truly mad. In the early 1980s, the combined U.S. and Soviet arsenals held more than 40,000 strategic (i.e. long-range) nuclear weapons.

With the collapse of the Soviet Union and the deterioration of the Red Army, attention shifted to safeguarding the Soviet warheads. In a remarkable piece of statesmanship, Congress funded the Nunn-Lugar Cooperative Threat Reduction program to secure and destroy surplus Soviet weapons on the ground. Spending about $8 billion from 1992 to 2003, the program deactivated about 6000 warheads and destroyed hundreds of missiles and silos as well as 97 bombers, 24 nuclear-armed submarines, hundreds of nuclear anti-submarine missiles, hundreds of submarine-launched missiles and their launchers and 194 nuclear test tunnels. Nevertheless, elements of the vast remaining Russian arsenal are poorly guarded and still offer tempting opportunities to any terrorist seeking to acquire a nuclear weapon.[121]

The Cold War established beyond argument the futility of an armed attack on a nuclear state by another nuclear state. Winning such a war would not be appreciably different from losing. But while peace was thus kept between the principals, their long struggle fueled civil wars throughout the world.

Meanwhile, the advent of nuclear weapons was followed by important changes in the social organization of that world. Some of these changes were affected by the new weapons; others had only indirect linkages or none at all. One momentous change was the conversion of European colonies and protectorates in Africa, Asia, the Pacific, and the Caribbean into independent nations. It had taken nearly 500 years for Europeans and their descendants to establish political control over nearly all of Asia, Africa and the Atlantic and Pacific islands.. Much of that control collapsed in barely thirty years, increasing the commonwealth of nations from about 50 sovereign states to nearly 200. The process had the tacit support of the both the U.S. and the U.S.S.R., which collaborated quietly on that single issue throughout the Cold War. Their own territorial acquisitions were mostly contiguous and those that were not had been incorporated into the national territory and went unchallenged. (France attempted the same procedure, unsuccessfully in Algeria but successfully in Guadeloupe and Martinique.) Britain retained a few insignificant colonial slivers from the empire of which it was said that the sun never set. South Africa, when independent, shook off a governing class of European descent. The U.S. undertook a second and more thorough emancipation of its African-American minority. China eventually reclaimed the ports of Hong Kong and Goa, held for so long held by Europeans. India achieved full separation from Britain and Pakistan seceded from India and Bangladesh from Pakistan. Most of the new nations were economically feeble at first but with the passage of time, China, India, South Korea, South Africa, Iran, Saudi Arabia and other newly enfranchised states became major players in a new global economy. The rapid abandonment of colonial claims was largely attributable to the military eclipse of the colonial powers—Britain, France, Spain, Italy, Belgium and the Netherlands - after World War II but also to the nuclear regime that provided better security for those nations than their lost overseas territories.

Between 1945 and 2005, the world's population increased from 2.4 billion to 6.5 billion, a rate of growth unprecedented in human history. The diffusion to developing countries of a few simple technologies—water purification, artificial milk, famine relief, antibiotics, electricity—sharply reduced their death rates without immediately affecting their high birth rates, and the numbers zoomed. By 2005, birth rates were falling in the poorest countries while some of the rich countries were facing an actual shrinkage of population. Deceleration had begun but the global population was expected to keep on growing for several decades more.

The settlement patterns of this vast horde were unlike anything seen before. In 1945, there were only 26 "urban agglomerations" with populations of a million or more in the world, most of them in Europe. By 2005, there were 438 of these huge centers, most of them in Asia. None were defensible against nuclear attack. All of them, for the time being, were uneasily sheltered by the nuclear taboo.

According to Paul Collier[122], there were 52 major civil wars between 1960 and 1999, lasting on average about seven years. Even in the poorest countries, a civil war requires the resources to arm and feed the government forces and the irregular forces that oppose them. The Cold War's contribution was to make arms and money available to both sides. As soon as one of the superpowers had identified its proxy, the other was automatically committed to the proxy's adversary. The government of any poor country with ties to either superpower was almost certain to face an insurgent movement armed and financed by the other. Since the end of the Cold War, drugs, diamonds, kidnapping and the governments of neighboring states have provided the sinews of war for civil strife in places like Colombia, Somalia, Sudan, Chechnya, Rwanda, Sierra Leone, Sri Lanka, Indonesia, Afghanistan and the Philippines.

The type of war that the League of Nations and the United Nations were founded to prevent—war between roughly equal national armies—began to go out of style with the advent of nuclear weapons. It makes no strategic sense for a nuclear state to attack another nuclear state. The potential costs outweigh any possible benefit. It makes even less sense for a non-nuclear state to attack a nuclear state or one that enjoys the protection of a nuclear-state.

Thus, although the United States and Russia still have thousands of nuclear missiles deployed against each other, no danger of attack is perceived by either. Although Syria, Saudi Arabia, Iraq, Iran and Libya remained hostile to Israel after the third Arab-Israel war in 1972, they have been deterred ever since by Israel's undeclared but unmistakable nuclear arsenal,

Although India and Pakistan have fought three wars and are still actively opposed over Kashmir, they are inhibited by their reciprocal nuclear threats from taking any serious hostile action.

Meanwhile, wars of the classic international type have become inconceivable for the nations of the European Union. Together, they enjoy the protection of the American, British, and French nuclear arsenals. Severally, they have nothing to gain by independent military action.

In sum, none of the imaginable wars between nuclear powers is likely to occur in the existing international system. This insight has been fully grasped by the governments and peoples of western Europe and explains their relative indifference to issues of national defense as well as their relatively weak military establishments. It is not yet acknowledged by the U.S. government, which continues to plan actively for wars with China, Russia and other nuclear powers, or by the American people, who still seem to locate themselves in the old international system that Hiroshima and Nagasaki changed forever.

Chapter Ten

Low-Intensity Conflict

The relative security provided by the nuclear rules is considerably reduced by the increased incidence of low-intensity conflict throughout
the world and the threat—still unrealized—of nuclear terrorism.

There are no nuclear rules for low-intensity conflict. That awkward
term, which first appeared in the 1980s, covers guerilla wars, terrorism and insurgencies—the overlapping varieties of armed conflict between national governments and irregular forces and among irregular
forces.

What guerilleros, insurgents and terrorists have in common is that
they use deadly violence without legal authority in the service of political objectives. Insurgents and guerilleros are invariably described as
terrorists by the legal authorities whom they oppose but are more likely
to describe themselves and their friends as patriots, freedom fighters,
heroes, martyrs.

Terrorism can be defined as deadly violence directed against noncombatants. A few terrorists, such as the Oklahoma bomber, Timothy
McVeigh, have been independent operators but most terrorists are
trained, equipped and assigned their missions by a government agency
or a political organization. There is also something that can be called
state terrorism, when a government directs deadly violence against its
own citizens. The original Terror of the French Revolution—the mass
guillotining of aristocrats and political adversaries in 1793 and 1794—
was the exemplar. There have since been many other instances, down to
the massacres committed in Darfur in 2005 and 2006 by agents of the

Sudanese government. By contrast, a government's use of deadly force against foreign noncombatants is not regarded as terrorism.

A typical low-intensity conflict pits a regular armed force equipped with tanks, planes, helicopters, artillery and sophisticated communications against irregular forces composed of small, shifting bands armed with assault rifles, grenade launchers, mortars, explosives and now, cell phones. The irregular forces may include women and children. Despite the regular force's advantage in technology, training, and logistics, the irregular forces often prevail. Money for arms and ammunition is essential but not hard to find. Islamic jihadists receive generous support from Saudi and Iranian sources. Drug money finances the reviving Taliban in Afghanistan. Kidnapping supports guerilla movements in Latin America.

Recruitment is the key to success for irregular forces.. African insurgents can get all the adolescent recruits they want with the offer of an AK47 and regular meals. The suicide bombers of Islamist movements may or may not count on the favors of posthumous virgins but they are powerfully motivated by the promise of posthumous celebrity. The adversary's overwhelming military strength is itself a strong incentive.

Although the nuclear states of the twenty-first century are protected by Rules One and Two from attack by the national forces of other states, whether nuclear or non-nuclear, their armed forces are still designed as if to repel attacks of that obsolete type. In practice, they are employed on quite different missions: to protect client governments, confront domestic and foreign insurgencies, and for regime change and peacekeeping in foreign lands.

Protecting a client state against a non-nuclear enemy is the easiest of these tasks, provided that the effort is supported by a broad international consensus. The first Gulf War restored the independence of Kuwait while costing the U.S. very little in dollars or casualties. The liberation of East Timor by predominantly Australian forces was initially successful. The Kosovo operation used NATO air power to halt an ongoing genocide with no NATO casualties at all.

Repressing an insurgency that has popular support is a much harder assignment. There are no successful examples, unless the costly draw achieved by the U.S. in Korea in the 1950s is so counted. The efforts of France in Algeria and in Vietnam led to outright defeat. The U.S. got nowhere with ten years of hard fighting in Vietnam. The Soviet Union was driven out of Afghanistan by an almost primitive insurgency.

Most of the European colonial possessions achieved independence after World War II by means of low-intensity conflicts. Some of these were barely contested. Others—as in Vietnam and Algeria—were long and bloody. Sub-Saharan Africa has seen some of the most persistent low-intensity conflicts of the post-colonial era—in Nigeria, Congo, Rwanda, Burundi, Ethiopia, Angola, Sierra Leone, Liberia—but other parts of the world have not been immune, as witness current and recent conflicts in Colombia, El Salvador, Nicaragua, Peru, northern Ireland, Spain, Serbia, Croatia, Bosnia. Kosovo, Indonesia, Sri Lanka, Kashmir, Mexico, among others. No end is in sight for the low-intensity conflict between Israel and the Palestinians.[123]

Van Creveld[124] observed that the low-intensity conflicts fought between 1945 and 1991 had greater political consequences than the numerous conventional wars that were waged during the same era. The only conventional war during that periodwhich resulted in the establishment of a new national entity was the 1948 war between Israel and its Arab neighbors. Meanwhile, more than a hundred new nations were brought into existence by means of low-intensity conflicts

What accounts for the paradoxical advantage of poorly armed and barely trained irregulars when they confront a well-equipped regular army? The phenomenon is not new—witness the British redcoats harried from Lexington and Concord by the Minutemen, or the wasting of Napoleon's Peninsular army by Spanish partisans, or the Norwegian resistance in World War II that forced the Nazis to maintain an occupation force in Norway larger than Norway's male population—but it has assumed new importance since 1945.

The success of irregular forces seems to be partly attributable to their lack of formal organization and heavy equipment. Unlike the regular forces, which must put most of their personnel into non-combat positions in order to maintain the formal organization and operate the heavy equipment, nearly all of the irregulars are combatants. That can more than level the playing field. A regular force is continuously visible while irregular forces can disappear into a supportive or intimidated population and emerge only at times and places of their own choosing.

But the greatest advantage of the irregulars may be their superior motivation, as instanced by suicide bombing. Soldiers enlisted in a bureaucratic army cannot be expected to match the zeal of fanatics eager for martyrdom.

As international wars began to go out of style, everyone concerned could read the rules posted on the mushroom cloud. When Israel became a nuclear state, its Arab neighbors could no longer hope to renew the wars of 1967 and 1973. But it soon became clear that Rules One and Two, which protect a nuclear state from attack by other states, do not apply to sub-national groups, against whom nuclear reprisals are impractical. Bombing, kidnapping and rocket attacks became the tactics of choice for irregular forces in contention with nuclear states. Inevitably, the enemies of nuclear states adopted those tactics.. As of this writing, the two leading nuclear powers both have large armies in the field fighting irregular forces with indifferent results.

By the summer of 2006, more than twenty-five hundred American soldiers and Marines had been killed in Iraq; thousands more had been gravely wounded. At least ten times as many Iraqis had suffered the same fates. The Russian forces in Chechnya have been even more heavily blooded. Although reliable casualty totals are not available for most years of the Chechen insurgency, nearly five thousand Russian soldiers lost their lives in that conflict in the single year of 2002. [125] The Chechen losses, of course, were much greater. These are the model conflicts of the opening years of the twenty-first century. In each of them a well-trained, well-equipped professional army confronts Muslim insurgents with minimal training and equipment, inflicts heavy casualties but comes off poorly.

There were precedents, of course, but in its current form, the peculiarly effective tactic of suicide bombing was developed and applied by Palestinians in their resistance to the Israeli occupation of the West Bank. It is inextricably bound up with the religious themes of jihad and martyrdom. Suicide bombing in Palestine is usually aimed at soft targets like school buses and restaurants. In Iraq and Chechnya, it has been adapted to hard targets like military convoys, though soft targets have not been neglected. A reliable military method for suppressing a suicide bombing campaign has yet to be discovered.

The irregular forces that currently threaten the United States and its allies are Muslim extremists committed to jihad, or holy war, against "Jews and Crusaders." Theirs is a cult of righteous death and they are able to recruit young men and women and train them to embrace martyrdom. This is not mainstream Islam but its historic roots go deep. The jihadists, whose best-known spokesman is the elusive bin Laden, are openly trying to ignite a religious war of Muslims not only against Christians and Jews, but against secularists, Hindus, Buddhists and other non-Muslims. That must necessarily be a low-intensity conflict. The Muslim world has no regular military strength to speak of but its potential for low-intensity conflict is almost unlimited. More than a billion Muslims occupy a territorial belt that runs more than halfway around the waist of the world, from Morocco to Indonesia. Every nation in that belt contains extremist elements. Islamic fundamentalism is a millenarian ideology that exhibits much the same fascination with violence as the totalitarian movements that infected Europe in the twentieth century. Moreover, the United States and most European nations harbor sizeable Muslim communities in which jihadists can hide.

Islamic fundamentalism has foundation texts that serve the same function as the Communist Manifesto and Mein Kampf, notably the Koranic commentaries of Sayyid Qutb. It has its recruiting agents in Wahabi preachers and teachers who fan out from Saudi Arabia. The movement emerged from the shadows with the overthrow of the Shah of Iran and the rise of the Ayatollah Khomeini, for whom America was the Great Satan. Islamic fundamentalism has its own version of utopia - the restoration of the Caliphate and the universal establishment of Islamic law, which as practiced in Saudi Arabia and Iran, is patriarchal and puritanical. The penalty for adultery is death by stoning. Women are subject to male authority all their lives. Alcohol is absolutely forbidden. There is not much room for accommodation with secular legal systems. Although the movement seems to be designed for the illiterate Muslim masses, it has been especially attractive to men at the margin between Islamic and western culture. The Saudis and Egyptians of the 9/11 attack were educated in Europe and lived extensively in the United States. Many of the suicide bombers have had western backgrounds and secular educations.

One observer concludes that:

> Islamism in its radical version of the present poses every imaginable danger. And it will go on doing so, borne aloft, even now on gushers of Saudi wealth; guided in some places by the unreformed Shiite mullahs of Iran; drawing on sophisticated thinkers and Koranic scholars; supported by officers in the Pakistan army and by Pakistan's secret police . . . not just bin Laden's international brigade but the several Palestinian groups, the Kashmiri irredentists, the Indonesian slaughterers of tourists, the

Malaysian terrorists, the Filipino terrorists, the East African slaughterers of still more tourists, and so forth from country to country „„with recruits and money pouring in, not only from Muslim countries but from Western Europe and from North and South America alike.[126]

So what is to be done? The experience of dozens of low-intensity conflicts suggests that regular military forces will not be able to administer a conclusive defeat to the jihadists. There will be locally successful operations but they are likely to attract more new recruits to the movement than the successful operations take out. Islamic terrorism may be persuaded to fade away if the right combination of carrots and sticks can be found. It cannot be defeated in the field.

Yet as noted in a previous chapter, the jihadists do not seem to be seeking nuclear weapons as eagerly as was expected. The possibility that nuclear deterrence may turn out to be effective in these low-intensity, high-stakes conflicts is a ray of hope in an otherwise bleak prospect.

Chapter Eleven

The Imperial Project

The Cold War ended when the Soviet Union abandoned the contest for global domination. With the shrinkage of the Soviet Union into the less ambitious Russian Federation and the downsizing of the Red Army, the United States seemed to have achieved the supremacy that had eluded all of the previous contenders for domination of the international system from the emperor Charles V in the sixteenth century to Adolf Hitler and Josef Stalin in the twentieth. While the Russians continued to intervene in conflicts within and between former member states of the Soviet Union, they disengaged from their world-wide military commitments.

The U.S. did not disengage. The military establishment built for the Cold War continued to expand on every continent. American servicepersons are currently stationed in nearly all of the world's independent nations. In a recent year, according to the Pentagon, the U.S. owned and operated 725 large military bases in 38 foreign countries, plus innumerable smaller bases, secret bases and bases hidden under flags of convenience. Since then, new U.S. bases have been established in Kuwait, Qatar, Oman. Israel, Afghanistan, Pakistan, Bosnia, Kyrgyzstan, and Uzbekistan and a chain of large new bases is said to be under construction in Iraq.

The Department of Defense is the richest government agency in the world. It spends $0.4 trillion a year or $14 thousand a second and has three million people on its payroll. It owns and operates 600,000 buildings on 30 million acres in 6,000 locations in 146 countries, as well as 550 public utility systems, hundreds of thousands of motor vehicles, hundreds of warships and more than 20,000 aircraft.[127] The margin of superiority is both human and mechanical. U. S. uniformed personnel, all of whom are volunteers, are better fed, paid, housed and equipped than those of any other nation. They are literate and thoroughly trained. They have more and better motor vehicles, earth-movers, helicopters, tanks, planes, boats, ships, guns, radios, computers and power tools than any other armed force. A fleet of huge cargo planes enables troops and supplies to be ferried anywhere in the world overnight. America's naval carrier groups rule the seas unchallenged: no other nation now has a fleet worthy of the name. All of this is topped off by almost inexhaustible supplies of ballistic missiles, cruise missiles, precision bombs and both conventional and nuclear warheads. No other government has anything like the same ability to inflict harm at a distance.

Joseph Nye compared the economic resources of the United States at the end of the twentieth century to those of its leading allies—Japan, Germany, France and Britain—and those of its leading potential adversaries—Russia, China and India.[128] The gross domestic product of the U.S. in 2000 was $9.3 trillion. The combined GDPs of the allies was $7.5 trillion, of the potential adversaries, $7.2 trillion. But the U.S. margin in 1999 military expenditures was much greater" $289 billion in 1999, compared to combined expenditures of $130 billion by the allies and $54 billion by the potential adversaries. The figures for military personnel are equally interesting: 1.4 million for the U.S.; 1.1 million for the two allies combined, 4.9 million for the potential adversaries.

From 1999 to 2006, U.S. military expenditures in real terms increased by more than 50 percent, widening the advantage. The expenditures of the other armed forces mentioned by Nye did not change much. The addition of new members to the European Union brought its total GDP up to parity with the U.S., while the GDP of China was about two-thirds as large and growing.[129] The European Union exceeded and China greatly exceeded the U.S. in population.

In relation to these competitors, the U.S. lost considerable economic ground between 1999 and 2006. Most Americans would be startled to learn that such familiar businesses as Holiday Inns, Texaco, the Chicago Sun-Times, Ben & Jerry's, Dr. Pepper, Brooks Brothers, Hellman's Mayonnaise, First Boston Investments, the Los Angeles Dodgers. Chrysler-Plymouth-Dodge and A&W Root Beer are now owned by Europeans or that the average American works longer hours for lower pay and benefits than the average European.[130] America's military superiority does not stem from overwhelming economic or demographic advantages but from a willingness to spend more on military equipment (including nuclear warheads) and to invest more in the individual combatant than any other nation.

U.S. military bases have been closed at the insistence of host governments in Greece, the Philippines and Spain. But U.S. military bases elsewhere have not been abandoned when their original missions disappeared. New missions can always be drawn from the bottomless well of national security.

The imperial pretensions came to the fore when the Soviet Union disengaged from the Cold War and the U.S. did not disengage. The Cold War seem to call for an American military presence in most of the world's countries and that presence, out of sight and largely out of mind, was not subject to any serious oversight. Bureaucracies do not surrender assets voluntarily and the Department of Defense is an especially powerful and well-insulated bureaucracy. The network of bases remained in place and continued to grow during the 1990s. But it still lacked an imperial mandate. The September 11 attack permitted the proclamation of such a mandate. It was set forth with admirable candor in *The National Security Strategy of the United States*, issued by the White House in September 2002, which claimed four major prerogatives for the United States: (1) to take preemptive military action anywhere in the world; (2) to intervene unilaterally in the internal affairs of other nations; (3) to suppress civil wars; (4) to prevent any other nation from rivaling the American military establishment.

Allies were to be cherished so long as they remained obedient. "In exercising our leadership, we will respect the values, judgment and interest of our friends and partners. Still, we will be prepared to act apart when our interest and unique responsibilities require." Nor was the empire to be limited geographically. "To contend with uncertainty and to meet the many security challenges we face, the United States will require bases and stations within and beyond Western Europe and Northeast Asia, as well as temporary access arrangements for the long-distance deployment of U.S. Forces."

Despite the enigmatic reference to Northeast Asia, China and Russia are not quite in the picture, and not quite out, rather like the Dacians and Parthians on the fringes of the Roman empire.

This was possibly the most consequential state paper issued by the U.S. government since the Emancipation Proclamation of 1863. Overnight, the American empire was transformed from a questionable metaphor to an empirical, if not quite constitutional, fact. In the *New York Times* a few months later, Michael Ignatieff rhapsodized:

> America's empire is not like empires of times past, built on colonies, conquest and the white man's burden. The 21st century imperium is a new invention in the annals of political science, an empire lite, a global hegemony whose grace notes are free markets, human rights and democracy, enforced by the most awesome military power the world has ever known.[131]

That was before the invasion and occupation of Iraq had shown that America's empire would in fact be built on protectorates, conquest and a version of the white man's burden.

The empire proclaimed with so much pride and confidence in 2002 looked much less impressive by 2006. The worldwide network of U.S. bases was still in place and still being enlarged. The missiles were ready in silos and submarines. The Pentagon still planned to achieve military superiority in space. But the invasion and occupation of Iraq had dispelled America's aura of invincibility. The distrust of the U.S. provoked by that occupation had made it more difficult to obtain cooperation from other nations and had provoked the two other "axis-of-evil" states to challenge the U.S. with nuclear programs for which no effective response had been found. In the few years since its publication, the imperial project made the United States disliked and feared throughout the world. According to a 2004 report:

> Even in the United Kingdom, the United States' most trusted ally, 55% see the U.S. as a threat to global peace. And in four EU countries—Greece, Spain, Finland and Sweden—the United States is viewed as the greatest threat to world peace, more menacing than Iran or North Korea, [132]

Even if U.S. and British forces eventually succeed in restoring order and establishing democracy in Iraq, the imperial project is unlikely to recover its luster. The chances are less than slim that the occupation will eventually turn profitable, that Iraqi children will again cheer the foreign soldiers, that oil revenues will reimburse American taxpayers, that democracy and the rule of law will flower in Baghdad and be imitated in Cairo and Riyadh.

Mounting domestic pressure suggests that withdrawal from Iraq may be fairly imminent despite the chain of new bases, the rhetoric of resolve and the unfinished business of reconstruction. The U.S. may yet negotiate a political solution and go home without waiting to see if it holds. Should that occur, there will be an opportunity to disengage not only from Iraq but from the imperial project. At base, it lacks a serious rationale. The nuclear rules make it unnecessary for the U.S. to be protected against any other national government. We will not be overtly attacked by any "rogue state" and although the same rules permit us to attack any non-nuclear state without a nuclear guarantor, the experiences of Vietnam and Iraq show the unwisdom of such actions. The U.S., military presence in other countries undoubtedly facilitates some of the business operations of American and multinational corporations but just as surely discourages others. Currently, the country's leading trade and investment partner is China, which has no U.S. military presence at all. The hundreds of billions of dollars that could be saved by a modest retreat from imperial pretensions would do far more for the American economy than imperial expansion. . Unlike all previous empires, from the Assyrians to the Nazis, America has not found a way to tax its foreign provinces and the cost of the imperial project begins to be seen as unbearable. Indeed, the *National Security Strategy* issued by the White House in March 2006 is far more modest than its predecessor, with a strong emphasis on international cooperation

The world-wide growth of the American military establishment has been both cause and effect of the militaristic attitudes now held by a large fraction of the American public.

> To state the matter bluntly, Americans in our own time have fallen prey to militarism, manifesting itself in a romanticized view of soldiers, a tendency to see military power as the truest measure of national greatness, and outsized expectations regarding the efficacy of force.[133]

One aspect of the new militarism is its links with evangelical religion and with the Republican party.[134] Such connections would have been unthinkable in the first two centuries of the American republic, when military service in wartime was an obligation of citizenship, supported by patriotic sentiments and enforced by conscription, while military service in peacetime had no political significance.

The founding fathers were famously anti-militaristic. "Overgrown military establishments are under any form of government inauspicious to liberty and are to be regarded as particularly hostile to Republican liberty, " said George Washington in his farewell address in 1796. Another great soldier expressed similar sentiments when he left the presidency in 1961:

> The conjunction of an immense military establishment and a large arms industry is new to the American experience . . . In the councils of government, we must guards against the acquisition of unwarranted influence, whether sought or unsought, by the military-industrial complex. The potential for the disastrous rise of misplaced power exists and will persist.[135]

The spirit of opposition to military establishments was faithfully observed from 1776 to 1948. For each of the nation's major wars during that period, a mass army was raised, trained, sent into battle and promptly disbanded with the coming of peace. The Union Army of 1866 had barely a tenth of its 1865 strength. The proportional shrinkage of the armed services after World War II was even greater. In the nuclear era the traditional pattern broke down. There was relatively little demobilization after Korea and even less after Vietnam when the low morale of the Army was cured by converting it to an all-volunteer force. That was good for the service in the short run but perhaps not good for the country in the longer run, as citizen soldiers responding to their country's call in the hour of danger were replaced by professional soldiers following orders.[136]

Yet it may not be coincidental that the U.S., which never lost a war under the old system of mass mobilization and rapid demobilization, has had less success under the new system. The record includes a drawn conflict with heavy casualties (Korea); a defeat with heavy casualties (Vietnam); and the tragic and costly occupation of Iraq.

On paper, the imperial project should be ripe for abandonment after a withdrawal from Iraq. The idea that the United States is entitled by its moral superiority and its nuclear arsenal to police the world and reform other nations unilaterally will have been tested and found wanting. The claim of moral superiority is not accepted by the rest of the world and the operational employment of the nuclear arsenal is blocked by the self-enforcing nuclear rules.

But this relatively happy prospect is shadowed by two difficult questions. First, can a large segment of the American public be persuaded to abandon the militaristic belief that might makes right when exercised by the right people. Second, can the present administration back away from its intermittent inclination to break the nuclear taboo?

Chapter Twelve

Post-Imperial Opportunities

The United States is still the world's sole superpower and likely to hold that title for many years to come. Under the self-enforcing nuclear rules, we cannot be seriously harmed by any other nation. Even the threat of terrorism is not acute so long as the nuclear taboo remains unbroken. Thus, into a future of unknown duration, the American government will enjoy an extraordinarily wide range of military, diplomatic and political options.

For the time being, those options are limited by the self-inflicted wound of the Iraq occupation and its ramifications throughout the Middle East and the world. When and if the U.S. disengages from that unhappy theater, it may rediscover the strategic freedom that a sole superpower should enjoy under the nuclear rules and perhaps use that freedom to strengthen nuclear restraints, buttress nuclear deterrence and reinforce the nuclear taboo, while engaging the jihadists with soft power and practical incentives. Those urgent purposes call for a discreet hegemony that favors persuasion over force and uses persuasion to strengthen the non-proliferation regime in every possible way. When the non-proliferation treaty began to be negotiated in 1965 it was expected that there would be 30 to 50 nuclear states by the year 2000. The non-proliferation regime must be credited with the fact that there are still only seven today, while 138 national governments have voluntary chosen nuclear abstinence.

The same strategic freedom would also permit the continuation of the neo-Wilsonian policy of encouraging constitutional democracy and market capitalism throughout the world, without the incompatible accommodations with tyrannical Muslim governments that the excessive involvement of the U.S. in Middle Eastern politics of the Middle East has seemed to require.

The exercise of hard power envisaged by the imperial project was sure to be widely resented and actively resisted. Fortunately, the U.S. still has in place the modalities for the exercise of soft power. Recent neglect has not damaged them beyond repair. A vast web of intergovernmental organizations ties the U.S. to its European and Asian allies and them to each other. In a 2002 issue of *Foreign Affairs*, Strobe Talbott presented a chart of "The Eurasian-Transatlantic Architecture." It included the European Union, NATO, the NATO-Russian Council, the NATO-Ukraine Commission, the Council of Europe, the Organization of Security and Cooperation in Europe, the Euro-Atlantic Partnership Council and eight other overlapping intergovernmental bodies in which the U.S. had either the leading role or significant influence.[137] The chart did not include the equivalent intergovernmental organizations in Southeast Asia and in Latin America, or the United Nations and its satellite organizations or such major economic institutions as the World Bank, the International Monetary Fund, and the World Trade Organization, all highly receptive to U. S. initiatives.

A sole superpower without imperial pretensions would be far more effective in encouraging the spread of constitutional democracy, political freedom and market capitalism around the world. And with its control of the seas and the air, it would still be able to protect populations threatened with genocide in failed foreign states. But for such actions to prosper, they must be acknowledged as legitimate by the people concerned and by third parties. The only presently available source of legitimacy is the "international community"—represented either by the United Nations or by regional consortia, like the five powers currently negotiating with North Korea.

The UN is admittedly a less than ideal world organization, but when it speaks with a single voice, it provides the only currently available source of legitimacy for armed interventions across national borders. That voice would be much stronger if the organization were to reform its membership rules and some of its administrative practices. The Security Council ought to be enlarged by the admission of permanent members as Germany, Italy, Japan and India; the reasons for their exclusion in 1945 are no longer remotely relevant. Half of the world's population and most of the world's resources would then stand behind the Council's actions. Membership in the General Assembly should be rearranged at the same time in order to reduce the ludicrous over-representation of micro-states whereby Tuvalu, with fewer than 12 thousand inhabitants, has the same single vote in that body as China, with more than 1300 million. The obvious solution was suggested by Winston Churchill in 1943 when he envisaged an international organization with small nations combined into regional blocs for voting purposes. On the administrative side, the most useful reform might be the conversion of UN office-holders into international civil servants, holding international passports and formally released from their national allegiances. This was perhaps the best feature of the old League of Nations. The Cold War prevented it from being carried over into the United Nations and the omission has created innumerable conflicts of interest within the organization. But even unreformed, the UN is the best source of legitimacy available to the United States for promoting nonproliferation and for intervening in the affairs of failed states—efforts that often overlap.

To be accepted as legitimate, such efforts must be genuinely cooperative, with substantial contributions of money, equipment and troops by a broad coalition of national governments. Cooperative operations under the aegis of the United Nations are vastly more affordable than unilateral incursions, as shown by the low cost of the first American-led invasion of Iraq and the high cost of the second.

The American commitment to democracy and political freedom is shared by all of the large developed nations—Britain, France, Germany, Italy, Japan and most of the smaller ones—Belgium, the Netherlands, Luxembourg, Switzerland, Norway, Sweden, Denmark, Finland, Spain, Israel, Canada, Australia, New Zealand and by several of the semi-developed nations of eastern Europe and of Asia. It is embedded in the structure of the European Union whose bill of rights is somewhat more extensive than that enshrined in our own Constitution.

Most of the world's nations currently describe themselves as democratic, including some, such as China, Zimbabwe and North Korea, whose citizens are conspicuously unfree. By one count, two-thirds of the world's countries currently have governments chosen by competitive elections; most of the others claim to be democratic in the sense of representing the popular will, although they have non-competitive elections or none at all.

But free elections alone do not create freedom. Democracy is meaningless without a framework of intermediate groups: political parties, voluntary associations, corporations, local authorities, together with a constitutional order that imposes respect for property rights and civil liberties, the separation of executive and legislative powers, independent courts and the rule of law. A system of free elections without these features does not offer much protection to unpopular groups or dissident viewpoints, and it contains the seeds of its own destruction, since a democratic electorate, unchecked by a strong constitutional order, can vote to abolish the democratic process.

It follows that the establishment of political freedom in a nation is a much more challenging task than the introduction of free elections. Besides the intermediate groups and the constitutional order, it seems to require a strong middle class, widespread literacy and a fairly high GDP. So far at least, there are no living examples of nations that enjoy freedom without these features nor any examples of poor nations that display all of these features. Although economic development does not guarantee political freedom, there can be no freedom without a solid economy.

For every South Korea in today's world, there are a dozen Haitis, weighed down by high fertility, poverty, illiteracy, disease and internecine violence. A half-century of foreign aid for the poorest nations has discredited most of the obvious development strategies. Emergency food relief is a palliative that does nothing to resolve the formidable cluster of problems that afflicts them. Large-scale industrial installations such as steel mills and hydroelectric dams fail with monotonous regularity in poor countries. Agricultural development projects are vulnerable to droughts, foreign competition, domestic corruption and the vagaries of commodity markets.

The foreign aid measures recommended by the experience of the past half-century are (1) the reduction of excessive fertility and (2) the suppression of armed conflict.

The reduction of excessive fertility is the easier task; significant reductions have already occurred in most of the poorest countries although not to the level that might enable them to break out of the cycles of poverty and violence. The education of women reliably reduces birth rates. Literate women have many fewer children than illiterate women; women who graduate from college have many fewer children than women whose education stops with high school. Subsidizing secondary and post-secondary education for women is the most effective way for the United States and its allies to nudge less advantaged nations towards the economic and social progress that can lead to political freedom.

Internecine armed conflict is endemic in the poorest countries. Besides causing famines and refugee flows, it blocks any general improvement in living conditions. The suppression of internecine conflict is the essential precondition to economic progress. It calls for massive and well-armed peacekeeping contingents and has become the most appropriate sphere of action for the armed forces of nuclear powers whose original missions of defending a national territory have been superseded by the nuclear rules.

Market capitalism is the other organizational form that the United States can legitimately propose to encourage elsewhere in the world. The emergence of an indigenous free market in a developing nation signifies that it is moving into the ranks of developed nations. By then it will have a large middle class, high living standards, general literacy and a full set of constitutional guarantees. It will necessarily admit foreign entrepreneurs on reasonable terms and participate in the global system of trade and currency exchange. Its politics will probably be democratic and its citizens will probably consider themselves free. It will not, if the nonproliferation regime endures, require or seek a nuclear arsenal.

Chapter Thirteen

Safer Than It Seems

Nuclear weapons, which are only useful if never used, have created a geopolitical world that looks much more dangerous than it is. With the disintegration of the Soviet Union, the threat of a nuclear war went from orange (with tinges of red) to bright green, or whatever color signifies relative safety, and there it remains to this day. But the American public, which lived quite comfortably with a plausible threat of nuclear war for forty years, now quakes at the thought of nuclear weapons in the hands of North Koreans or Iranians.

During the Cold War, both superpowers deployed thousands of nuclear warheads on hair trigger alert. Washington and Moscow took for granted the unrelenting hostility between them and the real possibility of having to absorb a first strike. Each understood that the first strike might be launched by accident or with deadly purpose, with equally catastrophic results.

Nothing like that looms over us today. The Russian Federation is a "strategic partner" of the United States although not always a comfortable one. The nuclear rules guarantee the immunity of nuclear-armed states from hostile national forces. The nuclear taboo remains unbroken and has just now, in the summer of 2006, survived a major test as the Bush administration backed away from a plan to use nuclear blockbusters in an attack on Iran's nuclear installations.[138] The five major nuclear-weapons states—the U.S., Russia, Britain, France, China—have no serious quarrels among themselves. The five proliferators or would-be proliferators—Israel, India, Pakistan, North Korea, Iran—show not the slightest disposition to attack any of the major nuclear-weapons states.

The classic problem of abolishing international war is nearly solved, although nobody seems to notice. What formerly seemed to call either for a world government or for a peacekeeping federation much more powerful than the United Nations, has yielded to the nuclear rules. For the first time in history, major geopolitical goals are being reached by international consensus with no application or threat of force. A striking example is the European Union, which has effectively abolished international war on the European continent, the historic theater of so many wars. Another is the voluntary adherence of nearly all the world's governments to the non-proliferation regime, along with the voluntary abandonment of nuclear-weapons programs by Libya, South Africa, Brazil, Argentina, Ukraine, Kazakhstan and Belarus. Compliance with the Limited Test Ban Treaty has been nearly perfect, and only the resistance of the United States and a handful of other holdouts has so far prevented its more comprehensive successor from coming into effect.

What all this signifies is that nuclear weapons have changed the normal relationships of sovereign states in a fundamental way. The nuclear-weapons states, being militarily invulnerable, have little to gain by going to war. Under the nuclear rules, they may not fight each other and their security is not enhanced by warring with non-nuclear states. Only the United States has chosen to do so, ostensibly, it must be remembered, to prevent Iraq from acquiring nuclear weapons and as of this writing, the United States government is threatening war against Iran for the same reason, although with less precipitation and more limited military resources.

If nuclear weapons could be wielded only by national governments, the present condition of the commonwealth of nations might well be celebrated as approaching the fulfillment of an age-old utopian dream — the abolition of international war. True, there are two kinds of international war that the nuclear rules permit: a conflict between non-nuclear states that have no nuclear guarantors and an attack on a non-nuclear state that lacks a nuclear guarantor by a nuclear state. There are only a handful of potential conflicts in the former category while the latter category contains only the United States and its axis-of-evil targets.

Of course, as the incidence of international war has declined towards extinction, the focus of fear has shifted to the possible use of nuclear weapons by terrorists and insurgents. Indeed, the U.S. invasion of Iraq was promoted as a precautionary measure against the possible transfer of nuclear weapons to terrorists by Saddam Hussein. Never mind that the Baathists and the jihadists had very different programs or that any such transaction might have invited a nuclear reprisal against the donor. The same concern is raised, with possibly more justification, with regard to North Korea. Pakistan, which has many more nuclear warheads than North Korea and with many jihadists in official positions, is seldom mentioned in this context, but the thought is there.

It would be foolish to deny the plausibility of the nightmare scenario in which a nuclear device transferred from a proliferator to a terrorist group is used to attack an American city. That would, of course, break the nuclear taboo and it would also unleash the full fury of an American nuclear reprisal against the suspected donor. So it may not happen. Another scenario would involve the transfer of a nuclear device to an insurgent group in Latin America or Africa. That too would break the nuclear taboo but would be less likely to provoke a nuclear response.

Terrorists and insurgents have been slow to leap at the nuclear opportunity, if indeed they see it as such, but unless they are contained, mollified or bought off, they may find it eventually. Meanwhile, the nuclear taboo remains unbroken and it is remarkable that a hypothetical nuclear attack on an American city arouses more apprehension today than a hypothetical Soviet attack on all American cities together aroused twenty or thirty years ago, although the means for the Soviet attack were in place and known to be adequate, while the means for a terrorist strike may not exist. This disproportionate reaction is probably attributable to the huge emotional impact of the September 11 attacks on the World Trade Center and the Pentagon. No sense can be made of today's geopolitics without taking account of the great fear aroused on that single day. The average American saw those frightening images over and over again and with strong encouragement from Washington, concluded that the enemy was not only implacable but irresistibly strong. Al Qaeda may indeed be implacable, but it has not been strong enough to mount another operation of the same importance and there is no reason to assume that it ever will be. While the threat

of nuclear terrorism remains potential, there is work to be done, both
here and abroad, in restoring America's reputation for good intentions
and good works and in reshaping our armed forces for a world in which
low-intensity conflict flourishes but international war is going out of
style.

Chapter Fourteen

Postscript

The preceding pages have set forth the reasons why I believe that the United States is not currently exposed to a military threat from any nation or combination of nations and why that happy condition might persist for many years. With much less confidence, I have also suggested that nuclear attacks on American cities by foreign terrorists may never occur.

Although the spontaneous appearance of the nuclear rules did not abolish "the war system of the commonwealth of nations," they changed that system by ruling out all the potential wars between nuclear-armed states and all the potential wars that might be initiated against nuclear-armed states by states without such weapons. Although many international wars were, and still are, permissible, the exclusion of wars between nuclear-armed states changed the war system in a fundamental way, by substituting bellicose postures for bellicose actions in the mutual relations of the world's most powerful governments. This situation created an opportunity to do away with international war altogether, but it has not been recognized or seized. Instead, the nuclear-armed states, with the United States in the lead, continue to envisage endless wars with each other and with non-nuclear states.

The nuclear rules have so far averted the threat of a general nuclear war, which might be out of scale with all other natural or man-made catastrophes. Remember that the U.S. was once prepared to launch a nuclear attack that was calculated to take 300 million foreign lives and to suffer an attack that would have killed 80 million Americans, and then reflect that the technical means to do such things and worse are still in place and ready to go. Other political issues pale besides this one. Mankind cannot breathe easy until nuclear weapons have been moved out of the center of human affairs. That cannot happen overnight, but while the nuclear rules and the nuclear taboo hold, there could be serious progress in that direction. It is remarkable that the two leading nuclear powers do not contemplate any reduction of their strategic nuclear weapons beyond 2000 on each side, while 200 could destroy either nation beyond repair. It strains credulity that they have not negotiated any limits at all on tactical nuclear weapons. Future generations may look back with amazement at the statesmen of the early twenty-first century who let so great a peril stand for no reason beyond bureaucratic inertia and a visceral attachment to obsolete military institutions.

Fission and fusion weapons cannot be uninvented. Nor can they be totally abandoned without grave risk. But it is possible to imagine a world in which a few responsible governments possess a few thermonuclear warheads stored separately from their delivery vehicles and open to universal inspection and perhaps, after many years of inactivity, the transfer of those dusty objects into the custody of a reliable transnational authority.

Notes

1. Henry L. Stimson. 1976. "The Decision to Use the Atomic Bomb." in B. J. Bernstein, ed. *The Atomic Bomb: The Critical Issues.* Boston: Little, Brown.

2. J. Robert Oppenheimer, Ernest Lawrence, Enrico Fermi, Arthur Holly Compton.

3. Stimson, quoted in Bernstein 1976, 8—a volume of collected papers reporting the arguments pro and con.

4. The long roster might be headed by Winston Churchill who urged the United States to attack the Soviet Union while it still had an atomic monopoly. Gaddis 2005, 65.

5. Described by S. Walker 2005, 299.

6. John Foster Dulles was one of the few exceptions. He would later promote the policy of "massive retaliation."

7. Clark 1985, 39.

8. J. S. Walker 2004, especially chapter 6.

9. For the details of the bottling by Arthur Compton and General Groves, see Walker 2005, 105-106.

10. op. cit.

11. He later abandoned this optimistic position. See Hershberg 1995 for the complicated development of Conant's nuclear views.

12. Ibid., 67.

13. Grant 1997, 290.

14. The principal source for this section is the biography of Oppenheimer by Bird and Sherwin 2005.

15. Ibid., 324.

16. Ibid., 332.

17. See Barton J. Bernstein 1983. "The H-Bomb Decisions: Were They Inevitable?" in Brodie, Intriligator and Kolkowicz. Chapter 16.

18. Damms 2002, 14.

19. Gaddis 2005, 63.-65.

20. From TomDispatch.com, 3/21/06.

21. National Security Archive 2006. *Newly Declassified Documents.* March.

22. Damms, 85.

23. April, 1956.

24. Although the Red Army had been reduced from about 11 million in 1945 to about 3 million in 1949.

25. Gray 1982.

26. *Statement of Secretary of Defense Before the House Armed Services Committee.* 18 February 1965, 69.

27. Allison 2004, 48-49.

28. Ibid., 12.

29. Ibid., 9.

30. Brodie 1946, 25.

31. Ibid., 48-49.

32. Ibid., 76.

33. Brodie 1945, 7.

34. Ibid., 89.

35. Ibid., 107.

36. Brodie. "The Development of Nuclear Strategy," in Brodie, Intriligator and Kolkowicz, 1983.

37. Brodie, 1971-72. "Why Were We So (Strategically) Wrong?" *Foreign Policy.* Winter.

38. Ibid., 160.

39. *Commentary.* 1977. 64:1:21-34, after Brodie.

40. It was until recently an exclusively male specialty.

41. *L'Arte della Guerra* 1521.

42. Ken Booth. 1975. "The Evolution of Strategic Thinking." in J. Baylis et al., *Contemporary Strategy: Theories and Policy.* New York: Holmes and Meier, p.35.

43. With a few British exceptions.

44. Schell 1982.

45. Gray 1984, 17.

46. Wohlstetter 1987, 16.

47. Herken 1985.

48. Kissinger 1957.

49. Kahn 1962, 1984.

50. In 1961, according to Daniel Ellsberg.

51. Bundy et al 1981, among others.

52. See, for example, Schell 1982, 1984, and Kennan 1982.

53. Perrow 1999, 3-4.

54. The principal source for this section is Tiwari and Gray 2005. As noted in that paper DOD has never released a complete list of accidents involving nuclear weapons but official sources refer to hundreds. Most of the particular incidents described by Tiwari and Gray date from the 1950s and 1960s.

55. Zuckerman, op. cit. 45.

56. Schram 2003. 99-101.

57. McPhee 1974.

58. Cited by Sublette 1999. Said to be detailed in a classified report UC-CRL-50248.

59. McPhee, 144.

60. Ibid.,, 225-226.

61. Cote 1996, 9.

62. Schram 2003, 21.

63. Allison 2004.

64. Ibid., 119.

65. A possible exception might be the unsuccessful attempt of members of the murderous Japanese Aum Shinrikyo cult to buy a uranium mine in Australia.

66. Benedetto 2005.

67. It is still possible to destroy an airliner in flight by smuggling an explosive aboard, but the fifty thousand federal employees who now search airline passengers are engaged in a largely symbolic exercise. Their procedures, together with the screening of baggage for explosives and the matching of baggage to individual passengers, offer protection only against the destruction of an airliner by a suicide bomber. Meanwhile, much of the freight carried by the same airliners is loaded on board without inspection.

68. Reiterated by President Bush in a news conference on April 28, 2006.

69. Electronic Encyclopedia of Civil Defense and Emergency Management, *Crisis Relocation Planning, 1974-1981.* (Accessed on the Web 5/20/06.)

70. More precisely, the arrangements for relocating "essential" government functions in a nuclear crisis continued to expand until the Soviet Union disintegrated, then were mostly shut down, then resumed on a larger scale after 9/11. See "Back to the Bunker," *Washington Post* 6/4/06, B1.

71. For further details, see Gaddis, 4.

72. Bruce Blair 2004. "Keeping Presidents in the Nuclear Dark." Retrieved from the Web at edi.org/blair. 2/16/06.

73. Department of Defense 2002. *Nuclear Posture Review [Excerpts].* January 8.

74. Department of Defense 2005. *Doctrine for Joint Nuclear Operations.* Joint Publication 3-12. March 15.

75. David B. Cloud. "U.S. prepares new rules on nuclear-weapons use." Retrieved from www.iht.com/articles/2005/09/11/news.nuke.php.

76. Hersh 2006b.

77. Ibid., 34.

78. Arkin 2006.

79. Hersh 2006a.

80. The title of an excellent but now outdated book on doomsday preparations by Zuckerman 1984.

81. *Washington Post,* 3/24/06, A17.

82. Theodore Caplow et al, Analysis of the Readiness of Local Communities for Integrated Emergency Management Planning (Federal Emergency Management Agency), 1983–84.

83. This section draws largely on Leebaert 2002.

84. Ibid., 242.

85. Zuckerman 11984. The incident is described in a footnote on page 332.

86. George Soros, internet communication, 13 June 2003, based on an article of his in *The American Prospect.*

87. The possible shape of that negotiation is fully explored by O'Hanlon and Machizuki 2003.

88. Wohlstetter 1987, called extended deterrence a "misleading notion." 30.

89. The principal sources for the following section are the web site of the Federation of American Scientists, and the texts of the respective treaties on the web site of the U.S. State Department, both accessed November 2005.

90. From the Preamble to the treaty.

91. Ibid.

92. Victor Mizin 2002. "The Treaty of Moscow" accessed from the NIT web site, November 2005.

93. For a history of the term "strategic" in connection with nuclear missiles, see Graffis 1994.

The term is sometimes used in a broader sense to include the aim of destroying an enemy's capacity to resist, but the narrower meaning is generally accepted.

94. It became effective in 1970.

95. Article IV, par. 1

96. Article VI.

97. There are several other multilateral nonproliferation agencies in which the U.S. participates without much public attention, including the Nuclear Suppliers Group, the Zanger Committee, the Missile Technology Control Regime, the Australia Group and the Wassennar Arrangement. Each of them monitors some aspect of the international trade in nuclear supplies, equipment and related technology.

98. Potter 2005.

99. Van Creveld 1991, 14.

100. Center for Defense Information. "The World's Nuclear Arsenals." 10/30/05

101. op. cit.

102. op. cit.

103. "Iraq: Countdown to showdown." 2005. *Bulletin of the Atomic Scientists.* October.

104. Stephen I. Schwartz 1998. *Atomic Audit: The Costs and Consequences of U.S. Nuclear Weapons since 1940.* From the Brookings Institution web site, 10/30/05.

105. Norris and Kristensen 2005.

106. In 2005, Russian representatives were invited to observe U.S. nuclear security tests in Wyoming and NATO observers were invited to Russian tests near Murmansk.

107. Center for Defense Information, 10/30/05.

108. Schwartz 1998, op.cit.

109. The principal source for this section is Center For Defense Information 2003.

110. Lewis 2005.

111. China's State Council 2005.

112. Afghanistan was a marginal case.

113. J. A. R. Mariott 1918. 74.

114. The legacy of the Brussels Declaration to later practice was the rule that a prisoner of war could not be compelled to disclose more than name rank and serial number.

115. As would be shown in 1914, when both the German and the French socialist parties abandoned international solidarity overnight to support the war policies of their respective governments.

116. For a fuller account see Stromberg 1982.

117. Sorokin 1962.

118. For a fuller account, see Dupuy and Dupuy 1986.

119. Brezezinski 1992. The quotation is from p. 10.

120. According to the Strategic Bombing Surveys conducted by the U.S. after the war, the urban bombing campaigns had little strategic yield.

121. A full account of the results of the Nunn-Lugar program and the continuing vulnerability of Russian nuclear forces and nuclear supplies is found in Schram 2003. See also Wolfsthal and Collins 2002.

122. Collier 2003a and.2003b.

123. Beginning with the overthrow of the Marcos regime in the Philippines in 1986 by massive street demonstrations, there have been a number of successful insurgencies of a new type in which oppressive regimes have been overthrown without bloodshed by massive popular demonstrations.

124. Van Creveld 1991, 21-22.

125. Johnson's Russia List 2003. Accessed on the web 11/27/05.

126. Berman 2002, 158-159.

127. Rocky Mountain Institute 2005. *RMI Solutions*. Fall, 5.

128. Nye 2002. Table 1.3, p.37.

129. Central Intelligence Agency 2005. *World Factbook*. November.

130. Reid 2004.

131. Ignatieff 2003.

132. Reid 2004, op. cit. 24.

133. Bacevich 2005, 2.

134. See Baker 2003 for supporting details.

135. Dwight David Eisenhower, farewell address, 17 January 1961.

136. One sign of this change is the abstention of elite youth from military service. According to Roth-Douquet and Schaeffer 2006, the number of recent Princeton graduates serving in uniform declined from 450 in 1956 to nine in 2004.

137. Talbott 2002. The chart is on p. 49.

138. Due to strong resistance from the Pentagon. The issue is fully described by Seymour M. Hersh 2006b.

Reference

Abt, Clark. 1985. *A Strategy for Terminating a Nuclear War.* Boulder CO: Westview Press.

Aron, Raymond. 1959. *On War.* Garden City, NY: Doubleday.

Allison, Graham. 2004. *Nuclear Terrorism: The Ultimate Preventable Catastrophe.* New York: Henry Holt.

Arkin, William M. 2006. "The Pentagon Preps for Iran," *Washington Post.* B1/B5. April 16.

Atkins, William M. and Richard Fieldhouse. 1985. *Nuclear Battlefields: Global Links in the Arms Race.* Cambridge, MA: Ballinger.

Bacevich, Andrew J. 2005. *The New American Militarism: How Americans are Seduced by War.* Oxford: Oxford University Press.

Baker, Kevin. 2003. "We're in the Army Now: The G.O.P.'s plan to militarize our culture," *Harper's Magazine.* October, 35-46.

Benedetto, Richard. 2005. "White House: U.S., Allies have foiled terror plots," *USA Today.* 15 October

Berman, Paul. 2003. *Terror and Liberalism.* New York: W.W. Norton.

Bernstein, Barton J. 1976. *The Critical Issues.* Boston: Little, Brown.

———. 1983. "The H-Bomb Decisions: Were They Inevitable?" in Brodie, Intriligator and Kolkowicz, Chapter 16.

Bidwell, Shelford, ed. 1978. *World War 3.* Englewood Cliffs, NJ: Prentice-Hall.

Bird, Kai and Martin J. Sherwin. 2005. *American Prometheus: The Triumph and Tragedy of J. Robert Oppenheimer.* New York: Alfred A. Knopf.

Boggs, Carl. 2005. *Imperial Delusions: American Militarism and Endless War.* Lanham, MD: Rowman & Littlefield.

Bogle, John C. 2005. *The Battle for the Soul of Capitalism.* New Haven: Yale University Press.

Boot, Max. 2003. "The New American Way of War." *Foreign Affairs*. July-August, 41-58.

Booth, Ken. 1975. "The Evolution of Strategic Thinking." in J. Baylis et al., *Contemporary Strategy: Theories and Policy*. New York: Holmes and Meier.

Bovard, James. 2003. *Terrorism and Tyranny*. New York: Palgrave.

Boyer, Paul. 1998. *Fallout*. Columbus: Ohio State University Press.

———. 1985. *By the Bomb's Early Light: American Thought and Culture at the Dawn of the Atomic Age*. New York: Pantheon.

Boyle, Francis Anthony. 1999. *Foundations of World Order: The Legalist Approach to International Relations (1898-1922)*. Durham, NC: Duke University Press.

Bracken, Paul. 1982. *The Command and Control of Nuclear Forces*. New Haven: Yale University Press.

Brams, Steven. 1985. *Superpower Games: Applying Game Theory to Superpower Conflict*. New Haven: Yale University Press.

Brezezinski, Zbigniew. 1992. *Out of Control: Global Turmoil on the Eve of the Twenty-First Century*. New York: Scribner

Brodie, Bernard. 1945. *The Atomic Bomb and American Security*. New Haven: Yale Institute of International Security.

———. 1946 "The Weapon." in B. Brodie, ed. *The Absolute Weapon: Atomic Power and World Order*. New York: Harcourt Brace.

———. 1959. *Strategy in the Nuclear Age*. Princeton, NJ: Princeton University Press.

———. 1971-72. "The Development of Nuclear Strategy." in Brodie, Intriligator and Kolkowicz 1983.

———. 1971-72. "Why Were We So (Strategically) Wrong?" *Foreign Policy*. Winter.

———. 1983. "The Development of Nuclear Strategy." Chapter 1 in Brodie, Intrilligator, Kolkowicz.

B. Brodie, M.D. Intriligator, and R. Kolkowicz, eds. 1983. *National Security and International Stability*. Cambridge, MA: Oelgeschlager, Gunn & Hain.

Bundy, McGeorge. 1988. *Danger and Survival: Choices about the Bomb in the first Fifty Years*. New York: Random House.

Bundy, McGeorge, George Kennan, Robert McNamara and Gerard Smith. 1982. "Nuclear Weapons and the Atlantic Alliance." *Foreign Affairs*. Spring.

Caplow, Theodore. 1989. *Peace Games*. Middletown, CT: Wesleyan University Press.

Carville, James and Paul. 2006. *Take It Back: Our Party, Our Country, Our Future*. New York: Simon and Schuster.

Center for Defense Information. 2003. "The World's Nuclear Arsenals." February.

Central Intelligence Agency. 2005. *World Factbook*. November.

Cote, Owen R., Jr. 1996. "A Primer on Fissile Materials and Nuclear Weapons Design." in Graham Allison and others, *Avoiding Nuclear Anarchy*. Cambridge, MA: John F. Kennedy School of Government.

China's State Council. 2005. *China's Endeavors for Arms Control, Disarmament and Non-Proliferation*. September.

Clark, Ian. 1985. *Nuclear Past, Nuclear Present: Hiroshima, Nagasaki, and Contemporary Strategy*. Boulder, CO: Westview Press.

Cochran, Thoms B. and others. 1984. *Nuclear Weapons Data Book. Vol. 1. Nuclear Forces and Capabilities*. Cambridge, MA: Ballinger.

Collier, Paul. 2003a. "The Market for Civil Wars." *Foreign Policy*. May-June, 38-45.

———. 2003b. *Breaking the Conflict Trap: Civil War and Development Policies*. Washington DC: World Bank.

Cronin, Audrey Keith. 2003. "Rethinking Sovereignty and American Strategy in the Age of Terrorism." *Survival*. 44:2, 119-140.

Daalder, Ivo and James M. Lindsay. 2003. *America Unbound: The Bush Revolution in Foreign Policy*. Washington DC: The Brookings Institution.

Damms, Richard V. 2002. *The Eisenhower Presidency 1953-1961*. Harlow, Essex: Pearson Education.

Department of Defense. 2002. *Nuclear Posture Review*. {Excerpts}. January 8.

Department of Defense. 2005. *Doctrine for Joint Nuclear Operations*. Joint Publication 3-12. March 15.

Department of Defense. 2006. *Quadrennial Defense Review Report*. February 6.

Dupuy, R. Ernest and Trevor N. Dupuy. 1986. *The Encyclopedia of Military History*. Second revised edition. Philadelphia: Harper and Row.

Ehrlich, Robert. 1985. *Waging Nuclear Peace*. Albany: SUNY Press.

Fallows, James. 2004. "Success Without Victory." *Atlantic Monthly*. January-February.

Feiveson, Harold A., ed. 1999. *The Nuclear Turning Point*. Washington DC: The Brookings Institution.

Flynn, Steven. 2004. *America the Vulnerable: How Our Government is Failing to Protect Us from Terrorism*. New York: Harper-Collins and Council on Foreign Relations.

Gergez, Fawaz A. 2005. *The Far Enemy: Why Jihad Went Global*. Cambridge, MA: Cambridge University Press.

Ford, Daniel. 1985. "The Button." *The New Yorker*. In two parts.

Gaddis, John Lewis. 2005. *The Cold War: A New History*. New York: Penguin Press.

Gallois, Pierre and John Train. 1984. "When a Nuclear Strike is Thinkable." *The Wall Street Journal*. March 24.

German Marshall Fund and Compagnia di San Paolo. 2003. *Transatlantic Trends 2003*.

Glaser, Alexander and Frank N. von Hippel. 2005. "Thwarting Nuclear Terrorism." *Scientific America.* 294:2:56-63.

Graffis, Judy M. 1994. "Strategic Use With Care." *Aerospace Power Journal.* Special edition.

Grant, James. 1997. *Bernard M. Baruch: The Adventures of a Wall Street Legend.* New York: John Wiley.

Gray, Colin S. 1982. *Strategic Studies: A Critical Assessment.* Wesport, CT: Greenwood Press.

———. 2003. *Maintaining Effective Deterrence.* U.S. Army War College: Strategic Studies Institute.

Hackett, General Sir John and others. 1978. *The Third World War: The Untold Story.* New York: Macmillan.

Halperin, Morton H. 1987. *Nuclear Fallacy: Dispelling the Myth of Nuclear Strategy.* Cambridge, MA: Ballinger.

Harvey, David 2003. *The New Imperialism.* New York: Oxford University Press.

Harwell, Mark A. 1984. *Nuclear Winter: Human and Environmental Consequences of Nuclear War.* Berlin: Springer-Verlag.

Hashim, Ahmed S. 2006. *Insurgency and Counter-Insurgency in Iraq.* Ithaca, NY: Cornell University Press.

Hentoff, Nat. 2003. *The War on the Bill of Rights.* New York: Seven Stories Press.

Herken, Gregg. 1985. *Counsels of War.* New York: Alfred A. Knopf.

Hersh, Seymour M. 2006a. "The Iran Plans." *The New Yorker.* April

———. 2006b "Last Stand: The military's problem with the President's Iran policy." July 10 & 17.

Hershberg, James G. 1993. *James B. Conant: Harvard to Hiroshima and the Making of the Nuclear Age.* Stanford: Stanford University Press.

Hoffman, Bruce. 2003. "The Legacy of Suicide Terrorism." *Atlantic Monthly,* June, 40-47.

Hoffman, F., A. Wohlstetter, D. Yost. 1987. *Swords and Shields: NATO, the USSR, and New Choices for Long Range Offense and Defense.* Lexington, MA: D.C. Heath.

Ignatieff, Michael. 2003. "The American Empire: The Burden." *New York Times Magazine.* January 5.

Jervis, Robert. 1984. *The Illogic of American Nuclear Strategy.* Ithaca, NY: Cornell University Press.

Kagan, Robert and William Kristol, eds. 2000. *Present Dangers: Crisis and Opportunity in American Foreign and Defense Policy.* San Francisco, CA: Encounter Books.

Kahn, Herman. 1982 *Thinking About the Unthinkable.* Pittsburgh, PA: Horizon Press.

———. 1984. *Thinking About the Unthinkable in the 1980s.* New York: Simon and Schuster.

Kaplan, Robert D. 2003. "Supremacy by Stealth." *Atlantic Monthly.* July-August, 66-83.

Kennan, George F. 1982. *The Nuclear Delusion: Soviet-American Relations in the Nuclear Age.* New York: Pantheon.

Kennedy, Robert F. 1971. *Thirteen Days: A Memoir of the Cuban Missile Crisis.* New York: W.W. Norton.

Kissinger, Henry. 1957. *Nuclear Weapons and Foreign Policy.* New York: Harper and Row.

Laird, Robin E. 1986. *The Soviet Union, the West and the Nuclear Arms Race.* New York: New York University Press.

Leaning, Jennifer and Langley Keyes. 1984. *The Counterfeit Ark: Crisis Relocation for the Nuclear Age.* Cambridge, MA: Ballinger.

Leebaert, Derek. 2002. *The Fifty-Year Wound: The True Price of America's Cold War Victory.* Boston, MA: Little, Brown.

Levinthal, Paul and Yonah Alexander, eds. 1986. *Nuclear Terrorism: Defining the Threat.* Washington DC: Pergamon-Brassey.

Lewis, Jeffrey. 2005. "The Ambiguous Arsenal." *Bulletin of the Atomic Scientists.* 61:3:52-59.

Litwak, Robert S. and Samuel F. Wells, Jr. 1988. *Superpower Competition and Security in the Third World.* Cambridge, MA: Ballinger.

Macrae, Norman. 1985. *The 2021 Report: A Concise History of the Future.* New York: Macmillan.

Mandelbaum, Michael. 2005. *The Case for Goliath: How America Acts as the World's Government in the Twenty-first Century.* New York: Public Affairs Press.

Mann, James. 2004. *Rise of the Vulcans: The History of Bush's War Cabinet.* New York: Viking.

McNamara, Robert S. 1986. *Blundering Into Disaster: Surviving the First Century of the Nuclear Age.* New York: Panther.

McPhee, John. 1974. *The Curve of Binding Energy.* New York: Farrar, Straus and Giroux.

Mariott, J. A. R. 1918. *The European Commonwealth: Problems Historical and Diplomatic.* Oxford: Clarendon Press.

Mosse, George L. 1990. *Fallen Soldiers: Reshaping the Memory of World Wars.* New York: Oxford University Press.

Nacht, Michael. 1985. *The Age of Vulnerability: Threats to the Nuclear Stalemate.* Washington DC: The Brookings Institution.

Norris, Robert S. and Hans M. Kristensen. 2005. "Russian Nuclear Forces 2005." *Bulletin of the Atomic Scientists.* 61:270-72.

Nye, Joseph. 2002. *The Paradox of American Power.* New York: Oxford University Press.

O'Hanley, Michael and Mike Machizuki. 2003. *Crisis on the Korean Peninsula: How to Deal with a Nuclear North Korea.* New York: McGraw-Hill.

Paret, Peter ed. 1986. *Makers of Modern Strategy: Machiavelli to the Nuclear Age.* Princeton, NJ: Princeton University Press.

Perrow, Charles. 1999. *Normal Accidents: Living with High-Risk Technologies.* Princeton, NJ: Princeton University Press. 2nd edition.

Phillips, Walter Allison. 1914. *The Confederation of Europe: A Study of the European Alliance.* London: Longmans, Green.

Pillar, Paul 2001. *Terrorism and U.S. Foreign Policy.* Washington DC: The Brookings Institution.

Potter, William C. 2005. "India and the New Look of U.S. Nonproliferation Policy." *Nonproliferation Review.* Summer.

Quinlivan, James T. and Glenn C. Buchan. 1992. *Theory and Practice: Nuclear Deterrents and Nuclear Actors.* Santa Monica, CA: RAND.

Reid, T.R. 2004. *The United States of Europe: The New Superpower and the End of American Supremacy.* New York: Penguin Press.

Robinson, Chalmers. 2004. *The Sorrows of Empire: Militarism, Secrecy, and the End of the Republic.* New York: Henry Holt.

Rocky Mountain Institute. 2005. *RMI Solutions.* Fall, 5.

Rosenbloom, Morris V. 1953. *Peace Through Strength: Bernard Baruch and a Blueprint for Security.* New York: Farrar, Straus & Young.

Roth-Douquet, Kathy and Frank Schaeffer. 2006. *AWOL: The Unexcused Absence of America's Upper Classes from Military Service—and How It Hurts Our Country.* New York: Collins.

Sands, Philippe. 2005. *Lawless World.* New York: Viking.

Schell, Jonathan. 1982. *The Fate of the Earth.* New York: Alfred A. Knopf.

———. 1984. *The Abolition.* New York: Alfred A. Knopf.

Schram, Martin. 2003. *Avoiding Armageddon: Our Future, Our Choice.* New York: Basic Books.

Shute, Nevil. 1957. *On the Beach.* New York: William Morrow.

Sorokin, Pitirim. 1962. *Fluctuations in Social Relationships: War and Revolutions.* Vol. 3 of *Social and Cultural Dynamics.* New York: Bedminster Press.

Soros, George. 2003. "Opening America's Views." *The American Prospect.*

Stromberg, Roland N. 1982. *Redemption by War: The Intellectuals and 1914.* Lawrence, KA: Regents Press of Kansas.

Sublette, Casey. 1999. *Engineering and Design of Nuclear Weapons.* Version 2.04. Retrieved from nuclearweaponsarchive.org, 10/6/05.

Talbott, Strobe. 2002. "From Prague to Baghdad: NATO at Risk." *Foreign Affairs.* November-December.

Tetlock, Philip E. and Aaron Belkin. 1996. *Counterfactual Thought Experiments in World Politics.* Princeton, NJ: Princeton University Press.

Tiwari, Java and Cleve J. Gray. 2005. *U.S. Nuclear Weapons Accidents.* Placed on the web by the Center for Defense Information.

Union of Concerned Scientists. 1987. *The Strategic Defense Initiative: Briefing Paper.* Cambridge, MA: Union of Concerned Scientists.

Van Creveld, Martin. 1991. *The Transformation of War.* New York: The Free Press.

Walker, J. Samuel. 2004. *Prompt and Utter Destruction: Truman and the Use of Atomic Bombs Against Japan.* Chapel Hill, NC: University of North Carolina Press.

Walker, Stephen. 2005. *Shockwave: The Countdown to Hiroshima.* London: John Murray.

Walt, Stephen M. 2005. *Taming American Power.* New York: W.W. Norton.

Wieseltier, Leon. 1983. *Nuclear War: Nuclear Peace.*

About the Author

Theodore Caplow, Commonwealth Professor of Sociology Emeritus at the University of Virginia, is the author of *Peace Games* (1989), and co-author of *Sociologie Militaire* (2000), *Leviathan Transformed* (2001) and *Systems of War and Peace* (1995, 2004).